VERB-INTENSIFIER COLLOCATIONS IN ENGLISH:
AN EXPERIMENTAL APPROACH

JANUA LINGUARUM

STUDIA MEMORIAE
NICOLAI VAN WIJK DEDICATA

edenda curat

C. H. VAN SCHOONEVELD
INDIANA UNIVERSITY

SERIES MINOR
NR. 86

1970
MOUTON
THE HAGUE · PARIS

VERB-INTENSIFIER COLLOCATIONS IN ENGLISH

AN EXPERIMENTAL APPROACH

by

SIDNEY GREENBAUM
THE UNIVERSITY OF WISCONSIN

1970
MOUTON
THE HAGUE · PARIS

221112

Printed in The Netherlands by Mouton & Co., Printers, The Hague.

To Masha and Avraham

PREFACE

This study is based on research conducted at the Survey of English Usage, University College London. The work was supported in part by a grant to the Survey by H.M. Department of Education and Science. I am grateful to Professor Randolph Quirk as Director of the Survey for providing the facilities for the experiments described in the following pages, and am also deeply indebted to him in a personal capacity for stimulus, advice, and practical assistance. To those who were my colleagues at the Survey thanks are due for acting as native informants or for giving practical assistance in connection with the experiments: Valerie Adams, Caroline Bott, Judith Carvell, Henry Carvell, Derek Davy, Norman Fairclough, Joan Huddleston, and Ruth Kempson. Caroline Bott also provided help on the statistical side. It gives me pleasure to acknowledge valuable comments on an earlier version of this study from Professor Barbara M. H. Strang, Sven Jacobson, Eddie Levenston, Jan Svartvik, and Eugene Winter. Particular thanks are due to Dick Hudson for his detailed criticism. Finally, I am conscious of the debt I owe to Geoffrey Leech, who gave a detailed reading to the first version of this work and offered many suggestions on both content and presentation.

University of Oregon,   SIDNEY GREENBAUM
Eugene, Oregon, U.S.A.
October 1968

CONTENTS

1

THE STUDY OF COLLOCATIONS

A complete linguistic description needs to take account of the restrictions on the collocability of one lexical item with another in
certain syntactic relationships, restrictions reflected in the deviance of the sentence *The boy may frighten sincerity* as contrasted
with the sentence *Sincerity may frighten the boy*. Restrictions of
this type can be defined in terms of the semantic features that are
assigned to the lexical items.[1] Other restrictions, however, cannot
be stated in general terms. It is then necessary to list the actual
lexical items that may collocate with a particular item. For example, *The man badly wished them to leave* seems deviant
though *The man badly wanted them to leave* is acceptable. *Badly*
(paraphrasable in this collocation by *very much*) is collocable
with *want* but not with *wish* or *desire*, synonyms of *want* (*cf.*
below, pages 62 ff.). It will be noticed that there is no syntactic
restriction on the collocability of *wish* with an intensifier, since if
we replace *badly* by *very much* the resultant sentence appears to
be acceptable: *The man very much wished them to leave*.

In addition to establishing the restrictions on collocability, we
may also wish to take account of the tendency for certain collocations rather than others to be likely in the language. Thus, we
may assume that there is some tendency for the word *stamps*, in
one of its meanings, to co-occur with such items as *collect, stick,*
and *post-office*. In such an investigation, we are dealing with

---

[1] On such restrictions, see Chomsky 1965, 148 ff., Matthews 1965, 35 ff.
For the term 'collocation' and some of its applications, see Firth 1957,
194 ff., Halliday 1966a, 18 ff., Halliday 1966b, 148 ff., McIntosh 1966,
183 ff., Sinclair 1966, 410 ff., Mitchell 1966, 335 ff.

probabilities rather than with absolutes, and the likelihood of a particular collocation will be affected by, among other factors, the subject-matter of the discourse and the level of formality.

1.1 CORPUS STUDY

One way of investigating collocations is to collect a corpus and to plot the patterns of collocations that appear in the corpus and their frequencies. The corpus may be restricted to one variety of the language or even to one variety of one idiolect (as in Behre's study of Agatha Christie's writings, discussed below), or, on the other hand, it may be selected to be representative of as many varieties of the language as can be conveniently differentiated and included.[2] Further, the field of investigation may be restricted to the collocation of a defined set of items with other items in the corpus or it may extend to all the overlapping patterns of collocation in the corpus. Finally, collocations can be studied independently of syntax or semantics in what may be termed the 'item-orientated' approach or the approach may be 'integrated'. In the integrated approach, collocations are studied with respect to the syntactic relationship between the collocating items and to the meaning of the items.

1.1.1 *An Item-orientated Approach*

An investigation of patterns of collocations in a corpus is envisaged in a programmatic article by Sinclair (1966, 410 ff.), which presupposes the aid of a computer. Unfortunately, the study, as envisaged in his article, would be based exclusively on linear co-occurrence of items, and would not include the syntactic and semantic statements that are often essential in a treatment of collocations.

---

[2]   A categorisation of varieties within a language is attempted in Gregory 1967. The bibliographical references in this article point to other attempts at differentiating varieties.

One major problem, for an analysis of collocations that is divorced from considerations of syntax, is that it does not seem possible to establish a criterion for determining whether two items are collocating. It is assumed that we can say that two items are collocating even when they are not immediately adjacent. Thus, *stamps* and *collect* can be said to collocate in all these three sentences:

They *collect stamps*.
They *collect* foreign *stamps* only.
They *collect* many things, but chiefly *stamps*.

We might even justify treating two items that appear in different sentences as collocating, *e.g.*:

They *collect* many things, though their chief interest is in *collecting* coins. We, however, are only interested in *stamps*.

The fundamental difficulty in the item-orientated approach is to decide the maximum distance between items that can be said to be collocating. This difficulty has been discussed by Halliday (1966b, 151-2) and Sinclair (1966, 414), both of whom wish to treat the study of collocations as a separate level of analysis. In such a treatment, the only solution that can be offered for this difficulty is the wholly *ad hoc* one of restricting the items to be considered as collocates to those that occur within an arbitrarily specified distance.[3]

A serious disadvantage of a purely item-orientated approach to the study of collocations is that it obscures syntactic restrictions on collocations. For example, *much* collocates with a preceding verb *like* in negative sentences but not in affirmative sentences. We can therefore say:

---

[3] The examples that we have given show that sometimes it is the stem of the item that enters into the collocation. *Stamps* collocates frequently with both *collect* and *collecting*, and, for that matter, *collects* and *collected*. On the other hand, this may not work the other way round. The singular form *stamp* is much less likely to collocate with *collect, collects*, and *collected*, though, of course, we have a frequent collocation in the compound *stamp-collecting*. *Cf.* Sinclair 1966, 419, Mitchell 1966, 337.

I don't *like* him *much*.

but not

**I *like* him *much*.

However, this last sentence becomes perfectly acceptable if *much* is premodified, *e.g.*:

$$I\ like\ him \begin{cases} very \\ too \\ so \end{cases} much.$$

Positional restrictions also apply. We can say:

Some people *much prefer* wine.

even though the sentence is in the affirmative. Yet *much* and *prefer* do not collocate if the intensifier is transposed to the end of the sentence:

**Some people *prefer* wine *much*.

A purely item-orientated investigation which excludes semantic analysis will encounter the problem of homonyms. For example, it might be found that *badly* collocates frequently with both *need* and *treat*, though in fact the *badly* that collocates with *need* and the *badly* that collocates with *treat* are two different lexical items, the first being an intensifier and the second a manner adjunct (see below, pages 25 f., 64 ff.). It is true that the two verbs collocate with overlapping but different ranges of nouns functioning as Direct Object. If therefore there is an adequate technique for the purpose it would be possible to show that only the intensifier *badly* collocates with *need* by establishing that there is a frequent collocation of *badly* with (for example) *money* and *drink* and that these nouns in turn collocate frequently with *need* but not with *treat*. But this procedure seems a roundabout way of establishing the frequency of the primary collocation, the intensifier *badly* and *need*, even if we assume the existence of the necessary computational technique. Moreover, there are sentences in which both the intensifier *badly* and the manner adjunct *badly* may enter, for example *He needed his friends badly* and *He treated his friends badly*. Such instances intensify the problem of assigning the collocations to one or other of the items *badly*.

1.1.2 *An Integrated Approach*

A more valuable, if more modest, contribution might be made to the study of collocations if a relatively homogeneous class of items were selected and an investigation undertaken of the collocation of each item in the class with other items that are related syntactically in a given way. A study along these lines has been undertaken by Behre (1967). Behre limits the scope of his enquiry to a few quantifiers and intensifiers: *a good (great) deal, a lot, lots, much, plenty, many,* and *a good (great) many*. He analyses in great detail the occurrences of these items according to the grammatical structures they enter and the items with which they collocate. Frequencies are listed for the quantifiers and intensifiers he has selected and for some other intensifiers by which they are sometimes replaced.

Behre rightly finds it necessary to justify limiting his study to the usage of one writer. He argues, 'firstly that the question of the usage of one writer (or informant) is a linguistic problem in its own right, secondly that the investigation of the speech-habits of one person (or informant) is the safest point of departure for every synchronic investigation in the field of syntax' (Behre 1967, 27). Nevertheless, he is aware of the disadvantages of such a limitation: a writer may have individual preferences and idiosyncrasies that will distort the results. On the other hand, he rejects the alternative method of corpus study, in which samples of writing are drawn from different writers, since, he argues, if our aim is to determine the habitual choice of each of the writers in a group, we cannot be sure that even an exhaustive sampling will give us frequencies that hold true for any one of them. It seems to me that this objection is valid only if we are interested in exact figures for frequencies. Significant differences, however, are likely to hold true if a large sample is taken from each writer.[4]

1.2 INFORMANT EXPERIMENTS

Instead of basing our investigations on a corpus of either written or spoken English, we can consult native informants. I shall outline and evaluate several procedures that may be adopted to elicit data on collocations. Since we shall be principally concerned with the collocation of verbs and intensifiers, the examples will be restricted to such collocations. The procedures may, however, be employed for other collocational studies. The types of test to be discussed comprise:

    (i) RECALL OF USAGE TEST: informants state which of one or more given forms of a sentence they habitually use;

   (ii) PREFERENCE TEST, having two components:

      a] RATING: informants evaluate the acceptability of two or more forms of a sentence;

      b] RANKING: informants state the order of their preference when given two or more forms of a sentence;

  (iii) EVALUATION TEST: informants evaluate the acceptability of a sentence;

  (iv) COMPLIANCE TEST: informants perform a simple grammatical operation on a sentence, the changes they may introduce in performing the task being noted;

   (v) COMPLETION TEST: informants complete a sentence, having been given part of it.[5]

---

[4] In the Preface to his work, Behre mentions that after his book was completed Agatha Christie produced a new story. He is encouraged to find that characters "follow the norm outlined at the end of Part I" and that "the omniscient narrator supports my statistics regarding the difference between narrative and dialogue". He does not draw the inference that it would have been possible to take a sampling of Agatha Christie's fiction-writing that would adequately represent her use of quantifiers and intensifiers.

[5] The experiments described in this study were conducted under the

1.2.1 *Recall of Usage Test*

To establish, for example, which intensifiers in final position collocate most frequently with the verb *like*, we might ask informants which of the following forms they habitually use:

He likes her *a lot.*
He likes her *a great deal.*
He likes her *a good deal.*
He likes her *much.*
He likes her *very much.*

The disadvantages of this procedure are perhaps obvious. In the first place, it is unlikely that informants will be able to recall with certainty which of the variants they actually use. Their replies will be even more suspect if they are asked to arrange them in order of frequency of use. Furthermore, their response may be influenced by what they think is preferable. An added complication is that the preferences they express may not reflect their true opinion, but may be influenced by memories, perhaps incorrect, of the precepts of parents and school-teachers. Or, indeed, they may be influenced by what are thought to be the preferences or expectations of the investigators. They may, for example, have been told at some time that *a lot* in this use is to be avoided, yet *a lot* may be their normal usage. When, however, they are asked to make a choice their awareness of prejudice against a variant may determine which item they select. Finally, the investigator may have failed to supply a form which is used most frequently by some of the informants. From all that has been said it seems clear that this procedure cannot be relied upon to give accurate information about usage.

This does not mean that the judgments of native informants, even when they do not coincide with their usage, are to be ig-

---

auspices of the Survey of English Usage. For a discussion of the techniques, see Quirk and Svartvik 1966 and Greenbaum and Quirk 1970. Analyses of the results will also be found in Greenbaum 1969a and Greenbaum 1969b.

nored. Linguistic opinions may, indeed, influence usage or impose restrictions on the context in which particular variants are used. Reaction to usage is a subject worthy of study, particularly when it can be correlated with evidence of actual usage.[6]

If we wish to know what informants think about variants we could employ the procedure we have been considering. However, the results would be vitiated for our purposes by the attempts of informants to recall their usage. Consequently, we could not draw any reliable conclusions about their opinions. If our aim is to elicit judgments, an explicit judgment test would be preferable.[7]

1.2.2 Preference Test

For this test we require informants to rate the acceptability of two or more forms of a sentence, all of which they have in front of them, and to rank them in order of preference. It has been thought advisable to present the sentences in duplicated form in a stapled booklet.[8] In the only experiment conducted with these tests the cover of each booklet contained the instruction: "Please do not turn over this page until you are asked to."

For the rating component a three-term scale has been found most useful, since it avoids the excessive polarisation that a two-

---

[6] Cf. the following observation by R. Quirk: "While it would seem obvious that natural usage provides by far the most valuable and important material for descriptive statements, I think one should aim at seeing educated usage as far as possible against the background of educated reaction (sic) to usage, a matter which is especially relevant perhaps for stylistic statements but by no means negligible for others. A distinction may further be made between 'believed usage' and 'preceptive usage'. What a person actually says may be different from what he believes he says, and this in turn may be different from what he thinks he ought to say." (Quirk 1960, 60).

[7] It has not been the practice of the Survey of English Usage to employ what I have termed the RECALL OF USAGE TEST. All the other tests discussed here have been conducted by the Survey.

[8] Oral presentation of two or more sentences with minimal differences may lead to confusion in the registration by the informants of their reactions, although reiteration of the sentences would reduce possible errors to some extent.

term scale enforces and the arbitrary distinctions that a more finely graded scale leads to.[9] In the wording currently employed at the Survey informants are asked to judge whether sentences are 'perfectly natural and normal', 'wholly unnatural and abnormal', or 'somewhere between'.

For the ranking component, informants were asked to write down against each sentence a number which would indicate the order of their preference. Thus, if there were three varying forms of the sentence, then the response '1' against a sentence signified 'most preferred'; '2', 'next preferred'; and '3', 'least preferred'. But it was permissible to respond with '1' for each of the three sentences if the three were liked equally, or with 'l' for two of the sentences and '2' for the remaining sentence, or with '1' for one of the sentences and '2' for the other sentences.

In the Survey experiment the set of preference tests came last in the Battery of tests and was preceded by the following instruction given orally:

Finally, one other task to do; this time you should use the stapled booklet in front of you. Each page contains two or three varying forms of a sentence. We should like you to look at these and make two judgments. First, make a snap judgment as to how normal and natural you find each sentence. As before, your answer should be given in terms of a three-point scale: *yes*, *no*, and *?*, and this has been written on each page as a reminder. Secondly, decide on the order of your preference for the sentences and then write down against each sentence a number corresponding to that order. You will see on the blackboard how the numbers are to be used. If you feel no strong preference, you may write down the same number for more than one sentence. This scale is written on the board to remind you of the possible reactions.

The scale for the ranking component was written on the board, with examples of possible answers, and a reminder of the available responses and their interpretation was written on each page for both the rating and ranking scales. The interval allowed for

---

[9] *Cf.* the discussion of this question in Quirk & Svartvik 1966, 10 ff., 46 ff.

writing down the responses was usually fifteen seconds, but twenty seconds were allowed when there were three sentences to be judged and also at the beginning of the set, to allow informants to become adjusted to the rhythm of the recurrence of sentences.

For variants, both judgments of preference and acceptability are necessary. If informants are asked merely to state the order of their preference, we could not know whether they regard all or some of the variants as unacceptable. On the other hand, if they merely evaluated the variants, we could not distinguish whether variants that have been accepted are in free variation, in their judgment, or whether there are preferences.

As with the recall of usage test, the responses for both the rating and ranking components may be influenced by what informants think they ought to say or what they think might be the expectation of the investigators. Hence, their responses may not represent their true opinion. However, this is likely to be a problem only if prescriptive statements have been made about the particular forms they are judging.

So far the preference tests conducted by the Survey have dealt with problems of number concord, the choice of auxiliary to be used with the negative, and orthographic variants. They have not been conducted with the intention of investigating collocations, but they could be used for this purpose.

1.2.3 *Evaluation Test*

For this test, sentences are evaluated according to the three-term scale adopted for the rating component of the preference test, but in this case one sentence at a time is presented for judgment and care is taken to distance within a Battery those sentences that exhibit similar linguistic problems. In the Survey experiments, the practice so far has been to record the instructions and Battery of tests on tape and relay them to informants. Thus, the evaluation test at present differs from the preference test in another respect: the test is given orally and not in writing. This is not, however, a necessary feature of the evaluation test, since it could be presented visually as well. For the preference test, on the other hand, visual presentation is more convenient, because of the complexity of the test.

After each sentence in a series of evaluation tests an interval of three seconds is left during which responses are written down. This interval has been found to be sufficient for a snap judgment.

A series of evaluation tests was conducted by the Survey to test the collocation of certain intensifiers with certain verbs. The tests were dispersed among other evaluation tests in two batteries. The collocability of four pairs of verb and intensifier was tested in three varying forms of a sentence. Two forms of the sentence were identical except that the intensifier was immediately preceding the verb in one form and at the end of the sentence in the other form. On the third occasion the sentence was transformed into the passive and the intensifier was positioned immediately before the passive participle. Thus, for the collocation tests on *completely manage* there were the three sentences:

his /sons *completely managed* the family bùsiness #
his /sons *managed* the family business *complètely* #
the /family business was *completely managed* by his sòns # [10]

The tests on the three sentences were designed to determine whether the collocability of *completely manage* was affected by the placement of the intensifier or by the voice of the verb. The results of these and similar tests are discussed in Section 4.

Evaluation tests may evoke responses different from those given in the rating component of preference tests on the same sentences. The rating in a preference test inevitably involves a comparison with other forms that are simultaneously presented, but such a

---

[10] For the system of notation, see Crystal & Quirk 1964. Only four features of the system appear in this study. The way they are marked is illustrated below in the environment of the word *sons*:
(1) the boundary of a tone unit: *sons#*
(2) the onset of a tone unit: */sons*
(3) a falling nuclear tone: *sòns*
(4) a level nuclear tone: *sōns*

comparison is not introduced into an evaluation test by the investigator, though informants may well be mentally matching the sentence with other possible forms. A difference in results from the two types of test has not been shown experimentally. However, it is reasonable to assume that informants will sometimes be more tolerant of less favoured forms when they are presented in isolation than when they appear in the company of more favoured forms.

Like the preference test, the evaluation test is designed to yield data on the attitude of informants rather than on their usage. With this type of test too, we may not be obtaining evidence of their true opinion if they respond in accordance with what they think is required or expected. However, in the tests on collocational problems to be discussed below, there is no reason to assume the presence of this distorting factor, since there do not appear to be any prescriptive rules that apply.

1.2.4 *Compliance Test*

The compliance test is a performance test in which informants are required to produce sentences. The test is designed to provide evidence of the informants' usage, though it may indicate a potential rather than a habitual usage.

The informants are asked to perform a simple grammatical operation on a 'test sentence', *e.g.* to turn the sentence into a question or to change the tense of the verb in a specified way. A mechanical performance of the task produces the 'target sentence'. If the 'response sentence', the sentence written down by the informant, is identical with the 'target sentence', it is registered as 'compliant', while if it deviates from the target sentence it is registered as 'non-compliant'. Target sentences that are unacceptable in some way may be expected to evoke non-compliant responses. Changes are introduced by informants in the course of re-creating the sentence with the required operation.

Compliance tests, corresponding to the evaluation tests, were conducted to test the collocability of the four pairs of verb and intensifier, once again in three varying forms of a sentence for each pair. The tests were dispersed among other compliance tests in two batteries that were recorded and relayed later at the experiment. The compliance tests were given before the evaluation tests so that informants should not receive the impression that they were being asked to evaluate the sentences. In each of the tests informants were required to change the tense of the verb, either from present to past or from past to present, depending on the tense of the verb in the sentence they were given. Thus, informants were given the sentence:

his /sons completely managed the family bùsiness#

and asked to turn the verb into the present. Both *His sons completely manage the family business* and *His sons are completely managing the family business* were regarded as compliant responses. Any response that deviated from these two forms of the target sentence was registered as a non-compliant response. The results of the compliance tests are discussed, and differences between them and the results of the corresponding evaluation tests are noted in Section 4.

One important advantage that compliance tests have over evaluation tests is that they supply indications of what caused dissatisfaction with a sentence. Informants may reject a sentence in an evaluation test for reasons that are irrelevant to the purpose of the test. For example, they may object to a sentence because they consider that what is said in it is untrue or improbable or that the particular sentence is unlikely to be said. At all events, we do not know what motivated their rejection of the sentence or their doubt about it. In the compliance tests, on the other hand, the unease or dissatisfaction that informants feel over a sentence may be pinpointed by the changes they introduce.

Compliance with the instruction in a compliance test is evidence of the informant's readiness to produce the target sentence when prompted to do so. This evidence can be construed as having a bearing either on actual usage or on potential usage. We should distinguish between the opinion of the informant about a sentence, his preparedness to produce the sentence, and his actual use of the sentence. It is not possible to generalise on whether compliance test results are related to actual usage or potential usage, important though this distinction undoubtedly is. With these particular tests, the results seem to be related to potential usage, since, intuitively, the collocations in the tests have a low frequency of occurrence.

Compliance tests have a limited usefulness in the study of collocations. They may be employed to focus on a particular problem, to determine the extent to which a particular collocation is objectionable. But they will only tell us whether the collocation will pass muster. They will not tell us whether it is an habitual collocation or to what extent it is preferred to other collocations.

1.2.5 *Completion Test*

This type of performance test was specifically devised to provide information on collocations and their frequency. In Survey experiments informants were given the instruction "Complete this sentence" and were given the opening words of a sentence, *e.g. the /man cērtainly*. Since the results of the completion tests are the main subject of this study, the design and evaluation of this type of test will be discussed in the following chapters in greater detail.

2

INTENSIFIERS

The term INTENSIFIER has been used here to designate certain adverbs that may be positioned before the verb. Semantically, these have in common some heightening effect on the force of the verb, but they differ among themselves both syntactically and semantically.

The completion tests reported on in this study were employed to determine the verbs that collocate with certain intensifiers in pre-verb position. It was also hoped to obtain information on the strength of their collocational link. It was expected that it would be possible, for at least some of the intensifiers, to establish semantic groups of verbs with which they collocate. The collocations may, of course, be different when the intensifier is positioned after the verb. The intensifiers selected for the tests were *certainly, really, badly, (very) much, greatly, entirely, utterly,* and *completely*.

2.1 INTENSIFIERS AND DEGREE INTENSIFIERS

Of the intensifiers that appear in the completion tests, all except *certainly* and *really* possess a semantic feature denoting extent. We can demonstrate this formally by making the intensifier the focus of clause negation and contrasting it with *to some extent* as the focus in a clause introduced by *but, e.g.*:

I don't need it *badly,* but I do need it *to some extent.*[1]

[1] If the verb group in the second clause does not already have an auxiliary, it is usually more acceptable if the emphatic auxiliary *do* is supplied. For the purpose of this test, the intensifier is positioned normally after the verb unless (as with *utterly,* for some informants) that position is felt to be unacceptable.

On the other hand, *really* will not contrast with *to some extent* in such a sentence as

    *I don't need it *really*, but I do need it *to some extent*.

Certainly cannot be tested for this criterion at all, since *certainly* cannot be included in clause negation, as can be seen from its unacceptability in the position immediately after the clause negative particle:

    *I don't *certainly* need it.

In this respect it contrasts with *really*:

    I don't *really* need it.[2]

The intensifiers that contrast in alternative negation with *to some extent* are termed 'degree intensifiers'. The degree intensifiers in the completion tests are *badly, (very) much, greatly, entirely, utterly* and *completely*.

    Certainly and *really* differ from the degree intensifiers in that they may appear before the auxiliary, *e.g.*:

$$\text{He} \begin{Bmatrix} \text{really} \\ \text{certainly} \end{Bmatrix} \text{will need it.}$$

They will even appear before the auxiliary when the clause is negated:

$$\text{He} \begin{Bmatrix} \text{really} \\ \text{certainly} \end{Bmatrix} \text{will not need it.}$$

The degree intensifiers are unacceptable in such positions, *e.g.*:

    *My friend *entirely* will agree.
    *They all *greatly* don't admire him.

As intensifiers *certainly* and *really* are distinct from what I call elsewhere the attitudinal disjuncts *certainly* and *really* (*cf.* Greenbaum 1969a). The attitudinal disjuncts *certainly* and *really* ex-

----

[2] For experimental evidence from informant tests to establish this distinction between *really* and *certainly*, see Greenbaum 1969a, 136.

press the speaker's conviction of the truth or reality of what he is stating. When they are positioned next to an item (usually in the same tone unit in spoken English, or when not separated by punctuation in written English), they appear to focus that particular item to such an extent that they are felt to be similar to intensifiers like *completely* or *utterly*.[3] Other items that function as attitudinal disjuncts and also may have an intensifying effect include *actually, definitely, indeed,* and *surely. Indeed* and *surely* are like *certainly* in not being included under clause negation. *Surely* is like *certainly* in that it is unacceptable in a question. All the degree intensifiers (and intensifiers like *actually, definitely,* and *indeed*) may appear within a question.

2.2 INTENSIFIERS AND MANNER ADJUNCTS

If we take the item *badly* as an example, it is an intensifier in the sentence:

He needs the money *badly*.

but a manner adjunct in the sentence:

He treats his servants *badly*.

Intensifiers may be distinguished from homonymous manner adjuncts by several criteria. First, only the manner adjunct can serve as a response to an interrogative transformation of the clause introduced by *How*. Thus, we have

How does he treat his servants? *Badly*.

but we cannot ask this question to elicit the response of the intensifier:

How does he need the money? **Badly*.

---

[3] For experimental evidence for the distinction that is being made, see Greenbaum 1969a, 132 f., 144.

Secondly, intensifiers are always fully acceptable before the verb in a declarative affirmative sentence whereas manner adjuncts often are not acceptable in that position (*cf.* pages 64 ff.). Thirdly, manner adjuncts can be paraphrased by a prepositional phrase in which the adjective base of the adjunct is inserted in the frame *in a —— manner* or *in a —— way.* Thus, we can say:

He treats his servants $\begin{cases} \text{in a bad manner.} \\ \text{in a bad way.} \end{cases}$

but we cannot say:

*He needs the money $\begin{cases} \text{in a bad manner.} \\ \text{in a bad way.} \end{cases}$

Finally, the intensifiers (apart from the special group containing *certainly* and *really*) contrast in alternative negation with *to some extent.* We can say:

He doesn't need the money *badly,* but he does need it *to some extent.*

but not:

*He doesn't speak *badly,* but he does speak *to some extent.*[4]

2.3 DEGREE INTENSIFIERS

The degree intensifiers are not identical in their syntactic and semantic features. To illustrate the differences, some sentences

---

[4] I have not applied the test to the sentence *He treats his servants badly* since in the normal interpretation of the sentence it would not be possible to replace *badly* by anything other than a manner adjunct. For *treat* with the meaning 'behave towards' a manner adjunct is obligatory. It is optional for *treat* with the meaning 'to give medical treatment to' and for *treat* with the meaning 'give a treat to', although for the latter a manner adjunct is probably unusual.

are given, each with a degree intensifier placed immediately before the verb, and they are tested against certain criteria. For further comparison, several sentences containing degree intensifiers not included among the completion tests are added.

(1) He *badly* needs the money.
(2) Some people *much* prefer coffee.
(3) They all *greatly* admire his work.
(4) They *fully* accept responsibility.
(5) They *thoroughly* disapprove of his methods.
(6) They *perfectly* understood the question.
(7) They all *utterly* hated the film.
(8) My friend *completely* forgot her name.
(9) He *totally* rejected the suggestion.
(10) My friend *entirely* agrees with you.

A number of criteria have already been mentioned for distinguishing degree intensifiers from other intensifiers or from manner adjuncts. The following primary criteria apply to each of the degree intensifiers that have been listed:

(1) It is acceptable when positioned before the lexical verb in a declarative affirmative sentence. Thus, the intensifier *badly* satisfies this criterion, but not the manner adjunct *badly* (cf. pages 64 ff.):

He *badly* needs the money.
*He *badly* treats his servants.

(2) It cannot appear before the auxiliary. Thus, *much* satisfies this criterion, but not *really*:

*Some people *much* would prefer coffee.
Some people *really* would prefer coffee.

(3) It cannot appear in initial position in a clause, *i.e.* preceding Subject, Verb, and (if present) Complement. Thus, *greatly* satisfies this criterion, but not *usually*:

Greatly they all admire his work.
Usually they all admire his work.

(4) When it is the focus of clause negation, it can be contrasted with *to some extent* as the focus in a clause introduced by *but*. Thus, *fully* satisfies this criterion, but not *really*:

> They don't accept responsibility *fully*, but they do accept it *to some extent*.
> *They don't accept responsibility *really*, but they do accept it *to some extent*.

(5) It cannot be the focus of a cleft sentence. Thus, *thoroughly* satisfies this criterion, but not *here*:

> *It's *thoroughly* that they disapprove of his methods.
> It's *here* that they disapprove of his methods.

(6) It cannot be the focus of *only* in initial position and allow in consequence Verb-Subject inversion. Thus, *perfectly* satisfies this criterion, but not *then*:

> *Only *perfectly* did they understand the question.
> Only *then* did they understand the question.[5]

(7) It cannot serve as a response to an interrogative transformation of the clause introduced by *How*. Thus, the intensifier *badly* satisfies this criterion, but not the manner adjunct *badly*:

> *How does he need the money? *Badly*.
> How does he treat his servants? *Badly*.

(8) It can be modified by *so* followed by Verb-Subject inversion and a correlative clause. Thus, *utterly* satisfies this criterion, but not *really*:

> So *utterly* did they all hate the film that . . .
> *So *really* did they all hate the film that . . .

---

[5] The degree intensifiers cannot be focussed by *only* in any position, e.g.:
> *They only* perfectly *understood the question*.

(9) It cannot be paraphrased by a prepositional phrase in which its adjective base is inserted in the frame *in a —— manner* or *in a —— way*. Thus, the intensifier *badly* satisfies this criterion, but not the manner adjunct *badly*:

*He needs the money in a bad $\begin{cases} \text{manner.} \\ \text{way.} \end{cases}$

He treats his servants in a bad $\begin{cases} \text{manner.} \\ \text{way.} \end{cases}$

I now list subsidiary criteria that serve to differentiate between the degree intensifiers:

(a) It can be the focus of clause comparison with the correlatives *as ... as*. Thus, *badly* satisfies this criterion, but there is some doubt over the acceptability of *entirely* in such a construction:

He needs the money as *badly* as he needs the time.
*My friend agrees with you as *entirely* as he agrees with me.

(b) It can be premodified by *However* to form the opening of a dependent clause. Thus, *thoroughly* satisfies this criterion, but not *entirely*:

However *thoroughly* they disapprove of his methods, they ...
*However *entirely* my friend agrees with you, he ...

(c) It can be premodified by *How* to form the opening of either an interrogative or exclamatory transformation of the clause. Thus, *greatly* satisfies this criterion, but not *totally*:

How *greatly* do they all admire his work?
How *greatly* they all admire his work!
* How *totally* did he reject the suggestion?
* How *totally* he rejected the suggestion!

(d) It can be the focus of clause comparison with the correlatives *more . . . than*. Thus, *greatly* satisfies this criterion, but not *utterly*:

> They all admire his work more *greatly* than they admire his character.
> *They all hated the film more *utterly* than they hated the book.

(e) It can be premodified by *very*. Thus, *badly* satisfies this criterion, but not *completely*:

> He very *badly* needs the money.
> *My friend very *completely* forgot her name.

The degree intensifiers in the ten sentences given on page 27 are listed below in Table 1. In this matrix table the subsidiary criteria (a)–(e) are set out at the head of the column. When an intensifier in the column on the left of the table satisfies a criterion, this is indicated in the appropriate cell by a '+'; when it fails to satisfy the criterion, a '—' is entered. A query denotes doubt whether the criterion is satisfied or not. The registrations are based on my reactions and those of two colleagues who acted as native informants. When a query accompanies another symbol, it indicates that our reactions varied.

A horizontal line is drawn under the set of the first three intensifiers to draw attention to the identical pattern of entries that they have. The pattern of entries for *badly, much,* and *greatly* would apply to most degree intensifiers. These include (to mention but a few) *bitterly, deeply, highly, profoundly, severely,* and *violently.*[6] The other seven degree intensifiers are ordered in the matrix table to display a gradience, that is a graded variation in the similarity and dissimilarity of the items. These degree intensifiers may denote the highest degree or extent, so that, for example, *fully* may be paraphrased by 'to a full extent'. Semantically, they may be re-

---

[6] Other degree intensifiers to which the same pattern would apply may be found in the lists of intensifiers given in Stoffel 1901, Borst 1902, Kirchner 1955, and Spitzbardt 1965.

garded, when used in this way, as superlatives. Nevertheless, as the table demonstrates, they may themselves be capable of being compared or modified for degree or extent. To a varying effect,

TABLE 1

Matrix Table for Degree Intensifiers

	a	b	c	d	e
1) badly	+	+	+	+	+
2) much	+	+	+	+	+
3) greatly	+	+	+	+	+
4) fully	+	+	+	+	?
5) thoroughly	+	+	+	+	?–
6) perfectly	+	+	+	?	–
7) utterly	+	+	?	–	–
8) completely	+	?–	?–	?–	–
9) totally	+	?	–	–	–
10) entirely	?	–	–	–	–

they are used to intensify the verb rather than to express primarily degree. Native speakers differ in their readiness to use some of them in the constructions that are registered in the table. This reflects both divided usage and the effect of prescriptive teaching. A diagonal line has been drawn to highlight the gradient. The queries along this line are a typical feature of a representation of gradience.[7]

The subsidiary criteria were selected to differentiate between the degree intensifiers with respect to their use as superlatives. They differ in other ways. For example, some native speakers (including myself) feel doubt over the acceptability of *utterly* in post-verb position, though others find that position for *utterly* fully acceptable. This fact is not irrelevant to our present discussion. It seems intuitively that the intensifying effect is more pro-

---

[7] For the phenomenon of gradience, see Bolinger 1961 and Quirk 1965.

nounced when the degree intensifier is in pre-verb position, while the superlative effect is more likely to be present when it is in final position. It is desirable to obtain sufficient evidence from informants to demonstrate this distinction.[8]

---

[8] I have not included among the illustrations of degree intensifiers those that are undoubtedly restricted to the position before the lexical verb, for example, *quite* as in *I quite agree with you*. It will be noticed that *quite* satisfies all the primary criteria except criterion (8) (the ability to be modified by *so*) and that it satisfies none of the subsidiary criteria. *Quite* in *I quite like her* is semantically a 'downtoner' and not a degree intensifier (*cf.* Stoffel 1901, 129 ff.). The downtoner *quite* does not satisfy primary criterion (4) (ability to contrast with *to some extent*, as shown by a construction in which it is the focus of clause negation). It is probable that the downtoner can only occur in a negative clause when the negation constitutes a denial of a previous statement.

COMPLETION TESTS: TECHNICAL ASPECTS

We shall now consider the design of the completion test and discuss some results that reflect on the technique.

3.1 PROCEDURE

For each completion test, informants were first given the instruction "Complete this sentence" and were then given the opening
words of a sentence, in each case the potential Subject of the
sentence followed by an intensifier. A silent interval of twenty
seconds was allowed during which the sentence was to be written
down.

The completion tests were inserted in batteries of performance
tests, and were separated from each other by a number of tests
requiring grammatical operations to be performed on sentences,
mainly compliance tests (*cf*. page 20). It was hoped in this way to
minimise the effect that one completion test might have on a
subsequent completion test.

For the registration of results, if the informant changed in any
way the opening words of the sentence his response was invali-
dated. All percentages in the tabulation and discussion of results
are worked out in terms of the valid responses. As a check that
informants had heard the opening words correctly, they were
required to write these down before completing the sentence.

To find out whether the Subject of the sentence influences the
selection of the verb, the same intensifiers were given in the
opening words of tests in Batteries IIIa and IIIb, but the Subjects

were changed. One intensifier, *much*, that was premodified by *very* in a test in Battery II was included without premodification in tests in Batteries IIIa and IIIb.[1]

3.2 INFORMANTS

All the informants were native speakers of English, and most of them were undergraduates studying at either London University or Reading University. The total number of informants for each Battery was:

> Battery II   179
> Battery IIIa   117
> Battery IIIb   70

Battery II was given to six groups:

Group 1: 31 informants, undergraduates at University College London, most of whom were in their second year studying for Honours Degrees in Geography, English, German, or Classics;

Group 2: 50 informants, undergraduates at University College London, all of whom were medical students in their first year;

Group 3: 26 informants, undergraduates at University College London, most of whom were in their second year studying for Honours Degrees in History or Geography;

Group 4: 17 informants, undergraduates at University College London, from various years and various departments;

Group 5: 21 informants, undergraduates at Bedford College, London University, all of whom were female, in their second year studying for the Honours Degree in English;

Group 6: 34 graduate teachers of English attending a course on the relevance of linguistics to English teaching held at the University of London Institute of Education.

---

[1] It was a fault in the design of the experiments that the Subject preceding *very much* was not retained in one of the subsequent tests with *much*.

Battery IIIa was given to five groups of first-year Honours under-graduates at London University:

Group D: 33 informants at Bedford College, most of whom were female, studying English, with a few studying German or French;

Group E: 22 informants at University College, all studying German;

Group C: 26 informants at Westfield College, most of whom were female, and most of whom were studying English;

Group B: 18 informants at University College, studying English;

Group A: 18 informants at University College, studying English.

Battery IIIb was given to one group of informants at Reading University, students taking courses in Linguistics. All but three were undergraduates in their first year, and most of them were also taking courses in various languages, mainly English, French, and German. The three exceptions were graduates in the first year of the M.A. in Linguistics course.

3.3   GENERAL RESULTS

Table 2 lists the 13 completion tests distributed among the three Batteries. It states the total number of valid responses for each test and the verbs that were PRINCIPAL COLLOCATES, *i.e.* those appearing in at least ten per cent of the valid responses.

Table 2 demonstrates that there is a strong collocational tie between the openings of some of the sentences and particular verbs. Thus, *I /bādly* triggered off the verb *need* in 113 informants (65 per cent) and the verb *want* in 49 informants (28 per cent), so that there was only a scatter of 13 other verbs (7 per cent) that were otherwise recorded. It is even more striking that *I en/tīrely* was followed in 82 per cent of the responses by *agree*, the only principal collocate for this test. It still needs to be established that the selection of verbs is primarily determined by the intensifier.

TABLE 2

Principal Collocates

	Total valid responses	
BATTERY II		
H1 the /man cērtainly	173	be 40 (23%); know 26 (15%)
H2 the /child rēally	165	be 49 (30%); love 16 (10%)
H3 I /bādly	175	need 113 (65%); want 49 (28%)
H4 your /friend very mūch	161	like 46 (29%); want 29 (18%)
H5 they /all grēatly	176	admire 78 (44%); enjoy 36 (20%)
BATTERY IIIa		
Ta1 I en/tīrely	108	agree 89 (82%)
Ta2 they /all ūtterly	103	hate 10 (10%)
Ta3 we /all mūch	87	admire 25 (29%); enjoy 18 (21%); appreciate 9 (10%)
Ta4 my /friend complētely	117	forget 38 (32%); ignore 16 (14%)
BATTERY IIIb		
Tb1 my /friend entīrely	68	agree 38 (56%)
Tb2 his /father ūtterly	69	despise 7 (10%); hate 7 (10%)
Tb3 /some people mūch	63	prefer 35 (56%); admire 11 (17%); enjoy 7 (11%)
Tb4 I com/plētely	70	forget 35 (50%)

(The verbs listed constitute at least ten per cent of the total number of valid responses for a particular test.)

3.4 INFLUENCE OF THE SUBJECT AND PREMODIFIER OF INTENSIFIER

The Subject affects the choices made later in the sentence. A simple instance is its effect on the selection of personal pronouns. Table 3 displays for each test the personal pronouns in the objective form that appeared in the responses. The numbers include pronouns that appeared after a second verb, as in "did not come to see ME", as well as those appearing after the first verb, as in "didn't do IT". The number of pronouns appearing after a second verb is, however, also noted in parenthesis after the comprehensive total. If we consider the tests in Batteries IIIa and IIIb, in which the intensifier is identical but the Subject is different, we see that a possessive pronoun in the Subject will influence the selection of objective pronoun later in the sentence. With *they /all ūtterly* (Ta2) only 14 informants (14%) chose to include *him* in the sentence, while with *his /father ūtterly* (Tb2) as many as 32 informants (46%) selected *him*. The predilection for *me* will also be noted in the tests with the opening words *my /friend complētely* (Ta4) and *my /friend entīrely* (Tb1), although for the corresponding tests, *I com/plētely* (Tb4) and *I en/tīrely* (Ta1), grammatical constraints prevent the selection of *me* after the first verb.[2] We also observe the large number of times that *you* appeared after *your /friend very mūch* (H4).

It is more relevant to the purpose of the experiment that the Subject may affect the selection of the verb, and this factor must be taken into account in assessing the influence of the intensifier on the choice of verbs. Several verbs that were listed in Table 2 for Battery IIIa are not on the list of principal collocates for Battery IIIb, and vice versa. Other verbs that appear on both lists recurred with rather different frequencies, while *prefer* with the high frequency of 35 (56 per cent) after */some people mūch* (Tb3) does not warrant to be included among the list of principal collocates after *we /all mūch* (Ta3), since it then only occurred 8 times (9 per cent).

Similarly, in using this test to determine the verbs that collocate with intensifiers we have to be aware that premodification of the intensifier may affect the selection of verbs. Thus, *like* and *want* are principal collocates of *very much* (H4), but appear infrequently after *much* in Ta3 and Tb3. There may well have been different results in, for example, the lists of collocates in Ta1 and Tb1, if instead of *I en/tīrely* or *my /friend entīrely* informants had been given *I /almost entīrely* or *my /friend almost entīrely*. With some intensifiers a change of Subject or premodification, where this is

2 The reflexive pronouns were rarely selected.

TABLE 3

Selection of Objective Pronouns

	Total responses	me	us	you	him	her	it	them	-self -selves	Total
BATTERY II										
H1 the /man cĕrtainly	173	5 (1)		3		1	7	1	1	18
H2 the /child rĕally	165	1		1	2		9		3	16
H3 I /bădly	175			1	4 (1)	1	10		2 (1)	18
H4 your /friend very mŭch	161	15 (1)		54 (14)	3 (2)	5	5	1	1	84
H5 they /all grĕatly	176	1		3	40	11	14		3	72
BATTERY IIIa										
Ta1 I en/tirely	108			43			1		1	45
Ta2 they /all ŭtterly	103	8			14	3	10 (3)		3	38
Ta3 we /all mŭch	87		1	7 (2)	12 (2)	4	6		1	30
Ta4 my /friend complētely	117	24 (1)			3	1	9 (1)			38
BATTERY IIIb										
Tb1 my /friend entirely	68	30		3			1		3	37
Tb2 his /father ŭtterly	69	5			32 (1)	1	7 (2)			45
Tb3 /some people mŭch	63	1			5	3	3			12
Tb4 I com/plētely	70			3	4	1	19		1	28

(The number in parenthesis, representing the number of pronouns appearing after a second verb, is included in the previous total.)

possible, may have no or little effect; with others it may influence the selection of verbs drastically. It would require a series of controlled tests to cater for all possibilities. Nevertheless, completion tests are valuable precisely for this reason, that they provide a relatively easy method of controlling the variables that affect collocations.

3.5 EFFECT OF ORDER OF PRESENTATION OF TESTS

The tests in Batteries II and IIIa were presented in two different orders. For Battery II Groups 1, 2, and 3 (totalling 107 informants) received the 50 performance tests in one order, whereas Groups 4, 5, and 6 (totalling 72 informants) were given the tests in a sequence corresponding to tests 26-50 and 1-25 of the original order. For Battery IIIa Groups D and E (with 55 informants) were presented with the 50 performance tests in the first order, whereas Groups C, B, and A (with 62 informants) were presented with them in a sequence corresponding to 25-1 and 50-26 of the first order. The tests in Battery IIIb, which correspond to the tests in Battery IIIa, were given in the first order. The tests were presented in two different orders because it was thought necessary to investigate whether the order in which tests were presented would affect the responses of informants. It will be recalled that the completion tests were not adjacent to each other in the Battery, but were separated by other performance tests.

Table 4 shows the effect of the variation in order on the selection of the principal collocates in Batteries II and IIIa. It will be observed that all the verbs that are listed as principal collocates for the whole Battery are also principal collocates for each of the orders – with three exceptions. The exceptions are *love* as a collocate after *the /child rēally* (H2), *hate* as a collocate after *they /all ūtterly* (Ta2), and *appreciate* as a collocate after *we /all mūch* (Ta3). It is significant that these three verbs are on the borderline for inclusion in the general list of principal collocates.[3]

[3] In fact, two of these verbs, *love* and *hate*, recur less than 10 per cent

Table 4 also includes three verbs having a frequency of 10 per cent or more in only one of the orders and not reaching this frequency for the whole Battery. They are *look* (10 per cent) for H1, *need* (11 per cent) for H4, and *prefer* (13 per cent) for Ta3. The verb with the highest frequency as expressed in terms of percentage is *prefer*. However, the total number of responses for test Ta3 is rather small in each of the orders and this factor inflates the percentages of verbs occurring in just a few responses. Thus, *prefer* occurs only 5 times in the first order, but nevertheless this number represents 13 per cent of the responses. There does not seem to be any justification for ascribing the different frequencies of this verb in the two orders to the variability in order. We should rather explain them as random differences between two populations. When a χ^2 test was applied to test the variation in the frequency of *prefer* against the frequency of other verbs in the two orders, it was found that $\chi^2 = 0.46$ on one degree of freedom. This is not statistically significant. (I am considering a level of at least 5% as significant in the discussion of results of χ^2 tests.)

However, one striking difference between the two orders may be explained by the variability in order. For Test H4, with the opening words *your /friend very mūch, need* is recorded 11 times (11 per cent) for the first order and only once (2 per cent) for the second order. The proportional difference between the two orders is much greater for this verb than it is for any other verb listed in Table 4. I would suggest that the far greater frequency of *need* in the first order may be accounted for by the fact that in that order the test followed Test H3, with the opening words *I /bādly*. As can be seen from Table 4, 69 per cent of the informants wrote down *need* after *I /bādly* in the first order. The frequency of *need* after *your /friend very mūch* may be influenced by the more highly motivated frequency of this response after *I /bādly*.

---

of the total number of valid responses, but are included among the principal collocates because the percentage is rounded to the nearest whole number.

TABLE 4

Effect of Order of Presentation on Selection of
Principal Collocates

	Order	Relative position of test	Total responses	
BATTERY II				
H1 the /man cērtainly	1	1	102	be 31 (30%); know 14 (14%); look 4 (4%)
	2	3	71	be 9 (13%); know 12 (17%); look 7 (10%)
H2 the /child rēally	1	2	99	be 33 (33%); love 4 (4%)
	2	4	66	be 16 (24%); love 12 (18%)
H3 I /bādly	1	3	105	need 73 (69%); want 25 (24%)
	2	5	70	need 40 (57%); want 24 (34%)
H4 your /friend very mūch	1	4	103	like 22 (21%); want 21 (21%); need 11 (11%)
	2	1	58	like 24 (41%); want 8 (14%); need 1 (2%)
H5 they /all grēatly	1	5	105	admire 48 (46%); enjoy 21 (20%)
	2	2	71	admire 30 (42%); enjoy 15 (21%)
BATTERY IIIa				
Ta1 I en/tīrely	1	1	55	agree 44 (80%)
	2	2	53	agree 45 (85%)
Ta2 they /all ūtterly	1	2	51	hate 4 (8%)
	2	1	52	hate 6 (12%)
Ta3 we /all mūch	1	3	39	enjoy 11 (28%); admire 9 (23%); appreciate 2 (5%); prefer 5 (13%)
	2	4	48	enjoy 7 (15%); admire 16 (33%); appreciate 7 (15%); prefer 3 (6%)
Ta4 my /friend complētely	1	4	55	forget 20 (36%); ignore 10 (18%)
	2	3	62	forget 18 (29%); ignore 6 (10%)

(For Battery II, 107 informants were presented with Order 1 and 72 with
Order 2. For Battery IIIa, 55 informants had Order 1 and 62 had Order 2.
The verbs listed are all those that constitute at least ten per cent of the total
number of valid responses in either of the two Orders.)

The two tests were separated by four compliance tests. We may assume that the effect of previous tests would be more marked in a Battery consisting of completion tests only. There are two possible effects. One, possible collocates may appear with a higher frequency because they have been suggested in a previous test, as in the example just cited. Two, possible collocates may appear less frequently because informants may wish to avoid repeating themselves. In order to ascertain in a particular series of experiments whether the order of presentation of tests affects the results, it is advisable to present the tests in one or more reorderings. It is, however, evidence of the reliability of the completion test that verbs with high frequencies in one order have similarly high frequencies in the second order. Thus, the verbs with the highest frequencies are *agree* for Ta1, with 80 per cent in the first order and 85 per cent in the second order, and *need* for H3, with 69 per cent for the first order and 57 per cent for the second order.

3.6   GROUP VARIATION

Battery II was presented to six groups and Battery IIIa to five groups (*cf.* pages 34 f.). It is relevant to investigate the reliability of the completion test in pinpointing collocates with high frequencies when the population receiving the test is small. Tables 5-12 list the number of times that the principal collocates for the Battery as a whole (*cf.* Table 2, page 36) appear in the responses for the individual groups. The percentages in brackets denote the proportions out of the total number of valid responses. Verbs that appear in a group as often or more often than a principal collocate are given at the extreme right, but such verbs are not recorded if the principal collocate does not appear at all or only once. Test Ta2 (*they /all ūtterly*) has not been included among the Tables, since *hate,* the only principal collocate in this test for the whole Battery, is the most frequent collocate in only one group, occurring even there only four times out of 23 responses (17 per cent), while in three groups it appears only once. For the point under discussion, this Test does not warrant inclusion.

TABLE 5

Frequencies of 'Agree' After 'I En/tīrely' (Test Ta1)

Group	Frequencies	Total responses
	agree	
D	27 (82%)	33
E	17 (77%)	22
C	21 (81%)	26
B	14 (93%)	15
A	10 (83%)	12

($\chi^2 = 1.70$ on 4 degrees of freedom. This is not statistically significant.)

TABLE 6

Frequencies of 'Need' & 'Want' After 'I /Bādly' (Test H3)

Group	Frequencies		Total responses
	need	*want*	
1	22 (76%)	5 (17%)	29
2	32 (64%)	16 (32%)	50
3	19 (73%)	4 (15%)	26
4	11 (65%)	5 (29%)	17
5	10 (50%)	9 (45%)	20
6	19 (58%)	10 (30%)	33

($\chi^2 = 9.46$ on 10 degrees of freedom. This is not significant.)

TABLE 7

Frequencies of 'Admire' & 'Enjoy' After 'They /All Grēatly'
(Test H5)

Group	Frequencies		Total responses
	admire	*enjoy*	
1	17 (57%)	4 (13%)	30
2	19 (39%)	10 (20%)	49
3	12 (46%)	7 (27%)	26
4	6 (38%)	4 (25%)	16
5	11 (52%)	2 (10%)	21 *hate*: 2
6	13 (38%)	9 (26%)	34

($\chi^2 = 6.67$ on 10 degrees of freedom. This is not significant.)

TABLE 8

Frequencies of 'Be' & 'Love' After 'The /Child Rēally' (Test H2)

Group	Frequencies		Total	responses
	be	love		
1	10 (33%)	1 (3%)	30	
2	12 (28%)	2 (5%)	43	cry: 3; know: 3; understand: 3; look: 2; hate: 2
3	10 (38%)	1 (4%)	26	
4	5 (33%)	2 (13%)	15	like: 2; hate: 2
5	5 (26%)	4 (21%)	19	
6	7 (22%)	6 (19%)	32	

($\chi^2 = 11.13$ on 10 degrees of freedom. This is not significant.)

TABLE 9

Frequencies of 'Like' & 'Want' After 'Your /Friend Very Mūch'
(Test H4)

Group	Frequencies		Total	responses
	like	want		
1	4 (13%)	4 (13%)	30	
2	12 (25%)	12 (25%)	48	
3	6 (24%)	5 (20%)	25	
4	5 (45%)	3 (27%)	11	
5	10 (71%)	2 (14%)	14	
6	9 (27%)	3 (9%)	33	dislike: 4; admire: 4; regret: 3; miss: 3

($\chi^2 = 25.19$ on 10 degrees of freedom. This is significant at the 0.5% level ($p < .005$). There is strong evidence of differences between the groups.)

TABLE 10

Frequencies of 'Forget' & 'Ignore' After 'My /Friend Complētely'
(Test Ta4)

Group	Frequencies		Total	responses
	forget	ignore		
D	15 (45%)	3 (9%)	33	
E	5 (23%)	7 (32%)	22	
C	6 (23%)	5 (19%)	26	
B	4 (22%)	1 (6%)	18	
A	8 (44%)	0 (0%)	18	

($\chi^2 = 16.09$ on 8 degrees of freedom. This is significant at the 5% level ($p < .05$). There is some evidence of differences between the groups.)

TABLE 11

Frequencies of 'Be' & 'Know' After 'The /Man Cērtainly'
(Test H1)

Group	Frequencies		Total responses	
	be	*know*		
1	10 (35%)	9 (31%)	29	
2	14 (29%)	2 (4%)	48	*do*: 4; *go*: 3; *walk*: 2; *run*: 2; *dress*: 2
3	7 (28%)	3 (12%)	25	
4	3 (18%)	3 (18%)	17	
5	1 (5%)	4 (19%)	21	*look*: 3; *like*:2; *go*: 2
6	5 (15%)	5 (15%)	33	

($\chi^2 = 20.75$ on 10 degrees of freedom. This is significant at the 2.5% level ($p < .025$). There is good evidence of differences between the groups.)

TABLE 12

Frequencies of 'Admire', 'Enjoy' & 'Appreciate' After 'We /All
Mūch' (Test Ta3)

Group	Frequencies			Total responses	
	admire	*enjoy*	*appreciate*		
D	4 (17%)	7 (30%)	2 (9%)	23	
E	5 (31%)	4 (25%)	0	16	
C	6 (33%)	4 (22%)	3 (17%)	18	
B	2 (13%)	1 (6%)	1 (6%)	16	*prefer*: 3
A	7 (40%)	2 (14%)	3 (21%)	14	*love*: 2

($\chi^2 = 20.18$ on 12 degrees of freedom. This is significant at the 10% level ($p < .01$). There is not sufficient evidence of differences between the groups.)

The verbs that are consistently the most frequent collocates are *agree* (Table 5), *need* (Table 6), *admire* (Table 7), and *be* (Table 8). The lowest frequency rates for these verbs are 77 per cent for *agree* (Group E, with 22 valid responses), 50 per cent for *need* (Group 5, with 20 responses), 38 per cent for *admire* (Group 4, with 16 responses, and Group 6, with 34 responses), and 22 per cent for *be* (Group 6, with 32 responses). On the evidence adduced so far we might assume that if the most frequent collocate has a frequency rate of at least 22 per cent in one group it will be the most frequent collocate in any other group. In other words, we might suppose that a frequency rate of 22 per cent or more for the most frequent collocate has predictive power.

However, other results show that the most frequent collocate in one particular group may have a frequency rate considerably higher than 22 per cent and yet not be the most frequent collocate in another group. Let us first consider Table 9, in which *like* is shown to be the most frequent collocate for all groups but two. In Group 2, with 48 responses, and in Group 1, with 30 responses, *want* and *like* have equal frequencies. Even if we discount the high frequencies of 45 per cent and 71 per cent for *like* in Groups 4 and 5 on the grounds that the total number of valid responses is very low (11 and 14 respectively) and that this factor skewed the results, Group 3 (with 25 responses) had a frequency rate of 24 per cent for *like* and Group 6 (with 33 responses) had a frequency rate of 27 per cent. Other results demonstrate even more clearly that a frequency rate of 22 per cent is far too low for the purpose we have been considering. We see from Table 10 that in Group D *forget* had a frequency rate of 45 per cent out of 33 responses. Nevertheless, in Group E *forget* appeared less frequently than *ignore*. Similarly, in Test H1 (Table 11) *be* had a frequency rate of 35 per cent in Group 1, with 29 responses, and yet had the same frequency as *know* in Groups 4 and 6, with responses of 17 and 33 respectively, and less than a number of other verbs in Group 5, with 21 responses. Similar differences between groups are shown in Table 12, but these may be explained by the small sizes of the groups.

It emerges that even if the most frequent collocate has a frequency as high as 45 per cent (*forget* in Group D, *cf.* Table 10) we cannot assume it will be the most frequent collocate in other groups, if our groups contain fewer than 50 informants. The Figure below is derived from Tables 5-12. It displays graphically the distance between the lowest and highest frequencies in individual groups for verbs that are the most frequent collocate in at least one group. (The variation for *prefer,* the most frequent collocate for Group B in Test Ta3, is omitted because the percentages involved are very small.) The greatest variation is for the verb *like* in Test H4, a variation of well over 5 per cent. However, we may account for this range, as we have said, by the smallness of the groups that registered the highest percentages (*cf.* Table 9). The ranges of the verbs that are consistently the most frequent collocate are generally narrower than the rest, as we might suspect.

Verbs may be consistently the most frequent collocate and yet the frequency need not be very high. The most obvious instance of this is the verb *be* after *the /child rēally.* This is the most frequent collocate for all groups, but its highest frequency rate is no more than 38 per cent (*cf.* Table 8). We shall have occasion to discuss the significance of this particular collocate when we consider the individual tests.

Despite the reservations that have been made, Tables 5-12 provide encouraging evidence of the reliability of the completion test in pinpointing frequent collocations. With only one exception, the verbs that appear most frequently in the groups are principal collocates for the whole Battery.[4]

The χ^2 test was used to test the variations between the groups in the frequencies of the principal collocates. The results (given in parentheses under Tables 5-12) show that the differences between the groups are not statistically significant for five of the eight tests, those on *I en/tīrely* (Table 5), *I /bādly* (Table 6), *they /all grēatly* (Table 7), *the /child rēally* (Table 8), and *we /all mūch* (Table 12). We are therefore left with three tests for which the differences between the groups have been shown to be statistically significant. For the test on *your /friend very mūch* (Table 9), it has already been suggested that the results of groups 4 and 5 may be affected by the low number of valid responses recorded

---

[4] The exception is in Group B for Test Ta3, with the opening words *we /all mūch,* in which *prefer* with three occurrences exceeds the two principal collocates (*cf.* Table 12). This verb has a frequency of 9 per cent for the whole Battery, just below the line we have drawn for principal collocates.

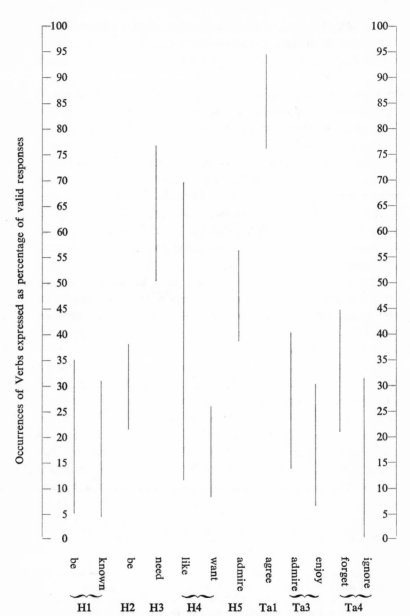

Figure: Lowest and Highest Frequencies for Verbs that are the
Most Frequent Collocates in at least one Group

for these two groups. The skewing effect of this factor would account for the difference between the groups. It must, however, be admitted that there are considerable differences in the frequency of *ignore* in the test on *my /friend complētely* (Table 10). But the differences are much less for the other principal collocate, *forget*, which is the most frequent collocate in four of the five groups. For the remaining test on *the /man cērtainly* (Table 11), the fluctuations between the groups are not surprising. It was not expected that any particular verbs would collocate with consistent frequency with the intensifier *certainly*. Inconsistencies between the groups were likewise expected for the test on *the /child rēally* (Table 8), since there was no expectation that particular verbs would collocate frequently with *really*. I shall argue later (pages 59 f.) that in the case of *be* the collocate is *be* with the following Complement, which together form an extended collocate. If we adopt this interpretation, then there are greater fluctuations between the groups for the tests with *certainly* and *really* than appear in the Tables for the principal collocates, since these are restricted to verbs.

4

EVALUATION AND COMPLIANCE TESTS:
LINGUISTIC DISCUSSION

I referred earlier (pages 18 ff.) to evaluation and compliance tests on four sentences, each given in three varying forms. The results of the evaluation tests are displayed in Table 13. They demonstrate a clear difference between the set *utterly expect* and the other three sets. All three forms of the sentence with *utterly expect* are rejected by informants. Lowest in acceptability is the active form of the sentence with *utterly* in final position. This suggests that for most of the informants *utterly* is restricted to pre-verb position when it is functioning in clause structure. However, confirmation for this restriction would require a test on a sentence in which *utterly* is acceptable in pre-verb position. This series of evaluation tests suggests that the collocation *utterly expect* is unacceptable.

The results present a more complicated picture for the other three sets, but for each the passive form of the sentence was not only accepted by a very large majority of the informants but also received a higher acceptance rate and a lower rejection rate than either of the corresponding active forms of the sentences. We may conclude that there is a greater acceptability of passive forms of sentences with the collocations *completely manage, entirely prepare*, and *fully observe*. Thus, the collocability of these three sets is influenced by the voice of the verb. The other difference that emerges distinguishes *completely manage* from *entirely prepare* and *fully observe*. In the active forms of the sentence there is little difference in acceptability whether *completely* is in pre-verb position or in final position, but final position is preferred for both *entirely* and *fully*.

Before the evaluation tests, compliance tests were administered to the informants. Table 14 records for each test the number and percentage of informants who complied fully with the instruction to change the tense of the verb in the way specified and made no other change. If we compare the results for the compliance tests with those for the evaluation tests we see at once that there is a greater range in the evaluation tests. Compliance totals in compliance tests range from 48 per cent to 92 per cent, while acceptance totals in evaluation tests extend from as low as 7 per cent to 93 per cent. It would seem that with respect to the sentences in these tests there is greater polarisation in attitude than in behaviour. There are a number of other differences between the results of the two types of tests. First, there are high compliance rates for the two sentences with *utterly* immediately before *expected*. Secondly, while in the evaluation tests *entirely* and *fully* are considerably more acceptable at final position than at preverb position, there is the same level of compliance for the two sentences with *fully* and there is actually the converse in the compliance tests on *entirely*.

If we turn to Table 15, we shall be able to see in detail some of the changes that were introduced. It is clear that the final position for the intensifier was more unacceptable, since informants transposed it more often when it was given to them in final position. The distinction is not so marked for *fully*, and is most marked for *utterly*. The omissions of either the verb or the intensifier or their replacement indicate dissatisfaction with the collocation. In only one sentence are there many such omissions and substitutions, in the sentence *his ar/rival was utterly expected by the stùdents ╪*. 39 informants (22 per cent) omitted or replaced one or both of the items *utterly* and *expected*. It is not clear why there were relatively few such omissions and replacements with the corresponding sentences in the active form. A complete list of the substitutions of verbs and intensifiers is given in Table 16. The only substitution to occur more than twice in a test is the replacement of *expected* by *unexpected* six times in test sentence G4 in Battery II. This is an interesting change, since *utterly* tends

TABLE 13: *Evaluation Test Results for Sentences with Intensifiers*

	+	—	?	No response
BATTERY I [85 informants]				
G1 his /sons *completely managed* the family bùsiness#	62 (73%)	10 (12%)	12 (14%)	1
G2 his /sons *managed* the family business *complètely#*	67 (79%)	12 (14%)	6 (7%)	
G3 my /friend *entirely prepares* the mèals#	48 (56%)	19 (22%)	17 (20%)	1
G4 my /friend *prepares* the meals *entìrely#*	69 (81%)	6 (7%)	10 (12%)	
G5 /our men *fully observe* Jòhn	50 (58%)	18 (21%)	17 (20%)	
G6 /our men *observe* John *fùlly#*	68 (80%)	7 (8%)	10 (12%)	
G7 the /students *utterly expected* his arrìval#	26 (31%)	38 (45%)	21 (25%)	
G8 the /students *expected* his arrival *ùtterly#*	6 (7%)	66 (78%)	13 (15%)	
BATTERY II [179 informants]				
G1 the /family business was *completely managed* by his sòns#	166 (93%)	6 (3%)	7 (4%)	
G2 the /meals are *entirely prepared* by my frìend#	158 (88%)	7 (4%)	14 (8%)	
G3 /John is *fully observed* by our mèn#	162 (90%)	3 (2%)	14 (8%)	
G4 his ar/rival was *utterly expected* by the stùdents#	53 (30%)	69 (39%)	57 (32%)	

TABLE 14: *Compliance Test Results for Sentences with Intensifiers*

	Total Compliances
BATTERY I [85 informants]	
G1 his /sons *completely managed* the family bùsiness#	63 (74%)
G2 his /sons *managed* the family business *complètely#*	64 (75%)
G3 my /friend *entirely prepares* the mèals#	75 (88%)
G4 my /friend *prepares* the meals *entìrely#*	65 (76%)
G5 /our men *fully observe* Jòhn#	57 (67%)
G6 /our men *observe* John *fùlly#*	57 (67%)
G7 the /students *utterly expected* his arrìval#	69 (81%)
G8 the /students *expected* his arrival *ùtterly#*	41 (48%)
BATTERY II [179 informants]	
G1 the /family business was *completely managed* by his sòns#	151 (84%)
G2 the /meals are *entirely prepared* by my frìend#	155 (87%)
G3 /John is *fully observed* by our mèn#	165 (92%)
G4 his ar/rival was *utterly expected* by the stùdents#	127 (71%)

TABLE 15: *Compliance Test Results – Omissions, Substitutions and Transpositions*

	Omissions			Omissions with Substitutions		Substitutions			Total	Transpositions of adverbs
	verb	adv	both	verb omitted with adv. replaced	adv. omitted with verb replaced	verb	adv	both		
BATTERY I (85 informants)										
G1 his /sons *completely managed* the family bùsiness#									0	3
G2 his /sons *managed* the family business *complètely*#									0	15
G3 my /friend *entirely prepares* the mèals#						1			1	6
G4 my /friend *prepares* the meals *entirely*#						1			1	16
G5 /our men *fully observe* Jòhn#		1	3						4	8
G6 /our men *observe* John *fùlly*#			2						2	11
G7 the /students *utterly expected* his arrival#		1	2				2		5	2
G8 the /students *expected* his arrival *ùtterly*#			3		1		2		6	33
BATTERY II (179 informants)										
G1 the /family business was *completely managed* by his sòns#		3			3	4			10	1
G2 the /meals are *entirely prepared* by my frìends#		1				5	3		9	1
G3 /John is *fully observed* by our mèn#	3		3	1		1			8	1
G4 his ar/rival was *utterly expected* by the stùdents#	3	1							8	1
	24				1	6	7		39	1

(With sentences in which the verb was in the past tense informants were required to turn the verb into the present tense, and with sentences containing a verb in the present they were required to turn it into the past.)

TABLE 16

Substitutions in Compliance Tests on Sentences with Intensifiers

---

BATTERY I (85 informants)

G1 *completely managed* – verb: 0; adverb: 0
G2 *managed . . . completely* – verb: 0; adverb: 0
G3 *entirely prepares* – verb: *propose*; adverb: 0
G4 *prepares . . . entirely* – verb: *propose*; adverb: 0
G5 *fully observe* – verb: 0; adverb: 0
G6 *observe . . . fully* – verb: 0; adverb: 0
G7 *utterly expected* – verb: 0; adverb: *certainly, absolutely*
G8 *expected . . . utterly* – verb: *await*; adverb: *soon, presently*

BATTERY II (179 informants)

G1 *was completely managed* – verb: *run* (2); *control*; *handle*; *carry on*; *own*;
ruin; adverb: 0
G2 *are entirely prepared* – verb: *make* (2); *provide; compare; compare;*
adverb: *completely*; *thoroughly*; *mainly*; *wholly*
G3 *is fully observed* – verb: *observant*; adverb: 0
G4 *was utterly expected* – verb: *unexpected* (6); *await* (2)
adverb: *fully* (2); *greatly* (2); *thoroughly*; *entirely*;
hourly; *absolutely*; *eagerly*

---

to collocate with verbs that have some 'negative' implication, as we shall see later (page 73). It is also interesting that some informants were prepared to make the substitution even though there is an agentive phrase introduced by *by* in this sentence. They thereby produced an agentful compound passive which does not allow an active transformation, since there is no corresponding verb **unexpect*.[1] Nevertheless, it is significant that only six out of the thirty-nine avoided the unacceptable collocation by the substitution of *unexpected*. This may well be because the others felt uneasy about retaining the agentive phrase with *unexpected* in the sentence:

---

[1] For an explanation of the fact that compound passives that have no corresponding verb form may occasionally be followed by agentive phrases, see Svartvik 1966, 162 and references given there. Svartvik quotes as an example of such a construction the sentence:

But Cavill was unimpressed by this sally.

His arrival was utterly *unexpected by the students.*

We could substantiate this explanation by repeating the test without the agentive phrase and noting whether a greater proportion of informants avoided the unacceptable collocation by the substitution of *unexpected.*[2]

[2] These evaluation and compliance tests were included in Batteries I and II. The composition of the groups of informants for Battery II is stated on page 34. Battery I was given to three groups of informants, all undergraduates in their first year at University College London:
Group 1: 29 students specialising in Geography;
Group 2: 29 students specialising in English Literature;
Group 3: 27 students specialising in Engineering.

5

COMPLETION TESTS: LINGUISTIC DISCUSSION

Before we begin an appraisal of the results of the individual completion tests, some statement should be made of how certain terms will be used.

A verb is termed a COLLOCATE of the opening words of a completion test if it appears as the main verb in the response of an informant. A particular verb is designated a PRINCIPAL COLLOCATE if it has a minimum frequency of 10 per cent of the valid responses for the whole Battery (cf. Table 2, page 36). The MOST FREQUENT COLLOCATE for a particular test is the principal collocate that appears more frequently than any other in the Battery, provided that for Batteries II and IIIa it is the most frequent in both orders (cf. Table 4, page 41). An OCCASIONAL COLLOCATE is a verb occurring in the responses with a frequency of less than 10 per cent. Some occasional collocates seem to be fully acceptable, even though they may appear only once. Thus, for Test H4 one informant wrote down *Your friend very much annoys me*. This is the only instance in which the verb *annoy* appears in a response after *your /friend very mūch*. On intuitive grounds, this seems a perfectly acceptable collocate.[1] On the other hand, some occasional collocates seem to be ABERRANT. For example, another informant responded in the same test with *Your friend very much has writer's cramp*. In this case, the collocation would be aberrant even if *very much* were in final position: *Your friend has writer's cramp very much*. But in the next example the deviance arises

---

[1] Where there was any doubt about the acceptability of collocations, colleagues were consulted.

from the position of *very much: Your friend very much thanked me. Very much* and *thank* collocate acceptably only when *very much* is positioned after the verb. The acceptability of this collocation is thus dependent on a syntactic factor.

In the ensuing discussion, reference will be made to individual collocates or semantic groups of collocates. These are listed for each test in the Appendix.

5.1 H1 *THE /MAN CĒRTAINLY* : H2 *THE /CHILD RĒALLY*

The intensifiers *certainly* and *really* differ from the degree intensifiers included in the other completion tests in that, intuitively, they collocate with any verb. The restrictions on collocability in the tests H1 and H2 are therefore to be explained as restrictions on the collocability of the Subject with the verb.[2] Nevertheless, the frequency of particular collocates in tests H1 and H2 might be influenced by the presence of the intensifiers *certainly* and *really*.

Of the large semantic groupings, items from two are hardly to be found outside the responses for the tests with *certainly* and *really*. The two semantic groupings are the one termed 'personal attributes' and the verbs of activity that are subdivided into groups of verbs of movement and crying and other verbs of activity. Together, the verbs in these groupings constitute over 60 per cent of the total responses for the test with *certainly* and nearly 47 per cent of the responses for the test with *really*. The absence of collocates of personal attribute in other tests may largely be accounted for by the fact that most of the collocates in this grouping are extended collocates (*cf.* page 60) containing the verb *be*, and the other intensifiers may not precede the verb *be*. As far as the

---

[2] For example, *The man certainly rained* is an unacceptable collocation unless a suitable Complement is present, *e.g. blows on the child*, but not *cats and dogs*. On the other hand, *It certainly rained* or *It certainly rained cats and dogs* are acceptable.

other grouping is concerned, we must simply say that verbs of activity generally do not collocate with degree intensifiers.[3]

Verbs that express an attitude of approval or disapproval on the part of the Subject towards the Complement or vice versa appear very frequently in the responses to several of the other tests (cf. Table 20, page 69). There are only ten such verbs in the test with *certainly*: the nine occurrences in the group of verbs of liking and disliking and the verb *astound*. Eight verbs that are principal collocates in other tests are not found among the collocates in this test: *want, agree, forget, admire, appreciate, prefer, despise,* and *ignore*. Three of these, *want, agree,* and *forget* are recorded in the Thorndike frequency count as occurring 100 or more times per million words, and two others, *admire* and *prefer,* as occurring between 50 and 100 times per million words. Furthermore, *want* is listed among the 500 commonest words in the Thorndike count (Thorndike and Lorge 1944). Seven of the eight principal collocates absent from the responses of the test with *certainly* are also absent in the test with *really*: *agree, forget, admire, appreciate, prefer, despise,* and *ignore. Want,* which is absent in the other test, appears four times in the test with *really.* The seven verbs may be absent from both the tests because they do not collocate as frequently with the Subjects of the two tests, *the man* and *the child,* as the other verbs that appear. However, it may well be that the verbs collocate less frequently with *cer-*

---

[3]   Items that are degree intensifiers in collocation with some verbs become quantifiers or frequentatives in collocation with other verbs (cf. Behre 1967, 66 ff.). We can contrast *He admires her a lot,* in which *a lot* can be replaced by *deeply, He goes to the theatre a lot,* in which it can be replaced by *often,* and *He drank a lot,* in which it is ambiguous, being either a quantifier or a frequentative. *A lot* as quantifier becomes the Subject in a passive transformation: *A lot was drunk (by him).* If there is already a Complement present in the clause, then *a lot* must be either a degree intensifier, as in *He admires her a lot,* or a frequentative, as in *He drinks beer a lot.* The exception is with verbs that take two Complements. In such cases *a lot* can be a quantifier, *e.g. He taught her a lot,* with one passive transformation being *A lot was taught her (by him).* In a private communication, Prof. Strang has pointed out that *a lot* can also be replaced by *a long time* in certain collocations. For example, in *He slept a lot last night, a lot* is durative.

tainly and *really*, possibly because there are in the language other pre-verb intensifiers that collocate frequently with these verbs. Further completion tests would presumably provide evidence as to which explanation is correct. For example, informants could be asked to complete a sentence with the opening words *the /mān*. They could then be asked to complete a sentence beginning *the /child cērtainly* or *I /cērtainly*. Most of the collocates after *the /man cērtainly* are appropriate only to an animate Subject, and two only to a human Subject, namely, *read* and *write*. It would be reasonable to assume that there would be different sets of verbs than we have had in the responses to this test if we were to ask informants to complete a sentence beginning */love cērtainly* or *the /dog cērtainly*. Undoubtedly many verbs found after *the /man cērtainly* will not appear at all with *love* as Subject, and others will probably occur that are not recorded. It is clear that *the man* has played a part in determining the collocate to follow *certainly*. What is not clearly established is whether *certainly* played any part as well. Similarly, in the test with *really*, some of the collocates would be abnormal if the Subject were *the man* instead of *the child, e.g. be mischievous, be naughty* (which occurred six times).[4] The influence of the Subject is even more evident if the whole of the informant response is taken into account. I quote a few clear-cut examples: *fell out of his cot, doesn't do well at school*, and *loves going to school*. Once again, further completion tests would show the part played by *really* in determining the choice of collocates.

Only *certainly* and *really* may precede the equative verb *be*.[5] The verb *be* is the more frequent of the two principal collocates after *the /man cērtainly*, with a frequency rate for the whole Battery of 23 per cent, representing 40 entries. It is the most frequent collocate with *the /child rēally*, with 49 entries (30 per cent) for the Battery. The verb *be* has a very light semantic load, and

---

[4] *Naughty* and *man* are sometimes collocated facetiously.
[5] The degree intensifiers may follow the verb *be*. For example, one informant, who did not conform with the instructions, produced the sentence *I am badly in need of medicine.* The term 'equative' applies to all uses of *be* except its use as an auxiliary.

it would seem justifiable to regard the following Complement as part of the collocate.[6] We would then, for example, take *be a fool* as an extended collocate (*cf*. Mitchell 1966, 342). We find further justification for this view in the synonymity or near-synonymity of some of the Complements. Thus, as well as *be a fool* we have *be foolish, be stupid, be crackers,* and *be insane*. For similar reasons, we may regard as extended collocates phrases containing the equative verb *look, e.g. look ill,* and, among others, phrases with the verb *have,* in at least some of its uses, *e.g. have a bald head*.

Some comment is called for on other verbs that appear a number of times in the responses to these two tests. We might suspect that after *the /man cērtainly* the high frequency of the verb *know* (occurring 26 times, 15 per cent) together with the 15 occurrences of the collocates classed as personal intellectual attributes can be ascribed to a collocational link with *certainly*. Support for this suggestion might be found in the fact that far fewer occurrences of the verb *know* appear after *the /child rēally*. I have cited above instances of collocates in that test which are appropriate to the word *child*. We might expect that there would, at the very least, be as many collocates in the class of personal intellectual attributes and as many occurrences of the verb *know* as in the test with *certainly*. Unfortunately, our results for the test with *certainly* may be contaminated by the compliance test that preceded it in the battery. The previous test had presented the sentence *she's /very clèver# be/tween you and I#* and had required the informants to negate the sentence. It may well be that in the absence of any strong collocational tie with other verbs informants plumped for a verb that was associated with the last sentence they were occupied with. The last sentence that informants were required to write down before this completion test was *She's not very*

---

[6] *Cf*. Lyons 1966, 219, who states of the verb *to be* in sentences such as *Mary is beautiful* and *Mary is a child* that it "may be regarded as a 'dummy carrier' of tense, mood, aspect and number in 'surface structure' (roughly comparable with the '*do*-auxiliary' in negative, interrogative and emphatic sentences).".

clever, between you and I. It is perhaps significant that in this test only three of the fifteen collocates in the class of intellectual attributes denote the presence of intelligence in the man, while in the test with *the /child really,* five out of the twelve ascribe intelligence to the child.

The number of occurrences of the verb *cry,* and its synonyms, is not surprising for a collocate of the Subject *child.* It is perhaps surprising, however, to find so many occurrences of the verb *love* and other verbs of liking and disliking. In only six of the 31 responses with these verbs is the Complement a personal noun (*hate* collocating with *his father* and *his mother, like* with *him,* and *love* with *his parents, her mother,* and *you*). Otherwise, the largest semantic set of nouns functioning as Complement refer to food.

Since degree intensifiers are normally unable to precede auxiliaries (*cf.* page 27 and the exception noted on page 71), we expect to find auxiliaries and clause negation only in the responses to the tests with *certainly* and *really.* After *the /man cĕrtainly* auxiliaries appear 37 times (21 per cent). Of these 27 (16 per cent) occur together with the clause negative particle: *did* (16), *is* (4), *was* (2), *does* (1), *is going to* (1) and *can* (1). The relatively great frequency of *did not* and *didn't* is worthy of note. It accompanies nine different verbs and once appears without the lexical verb. Only with one verb, *know,* does it appear as many as three times. The auxiliaries without the clause negative particle were *can* (6), *should* (1), *was* (1), and emphatic *did* (1). 34 auxiliaries appear after *the /child rēally,* a percentage of 21, exactly the same as for the test with *certainly.* Of these, 22 (13 per cent), co-occur with the clause negative particle: *did* (4), *does* (5), *would* (1), *should* (3), *can* (3), *could* (5), and *was* (1). We may point to the frequency of the modal auxiliaries in colligation with the negative particle for this test as contrasted with the test with *certainly.* The other auxiliaries were: *did* (2), *does* (2), *had* (1), *should* (2), *must* (2), and *ought* (2). The modal auxiliaries appear 18 times (11 per cent) in this test as compared with the 8 occurrences of modal auxiliaries in the test with *certainly* (5 per cent), which suggests that *really* has a greater tendency to colligate with the modal auxiliaries than *certainly* has, although it is possible that the Subject *child* may have some influence in this respect.

5.2   H3 *I* /*BĀDLY*

After *I* /*bādly* the two principal collocates are *need* and *want,* with *need* as the most frequent collocate. We have independent evidence that these two verbs are frequent collocates of the intensifier *badly*: the OED records that *badly* with the meaning 'much, greatly' occurs with *need* and *want*. It adds that it is used colloquially with these verbs. The information that *badly* is restricted to colloquial usage may help to explain why it does not collocate with verbs that occur with similar meaning in more formal usage, *e.g. require, desire,* and *wish.*[7]

In only four out of the 113 occurrences of *need* is it followed by an infinitive construction, in all cases with the *to*-infinitive: *to get out of here, to rest, to listen more carefully to English people, to buy another.* In contrast, *want* is followed by a *to*-infinitive construction in 30 of the 49 occurrences of this verb. It therefore seems clear that *badly* collocates frequently with the transitive verb *need,* as in *I badly need a drink,* and infrequently with *need* when it represents 'non-final elements in complex verbal phrases' (Svartvik 1968, 130), as in *I badly need to drink.* Even so, *badly* is collocable only with the non-transitive *need* that is followed by a *to*-infinitive construction. It cannot collocate with the 'auxiliary' *need,* which is followed by a *to*-less infinitive, *cf.* the distinction drawn in Svartvik 1968. Thus, we can contrast:

> He badly needs to wash.
> *He badly need not wash.
> *He badly need wash only in summer.

Badly does not collocate with *need* and *want* in some other uses.

---

[7]   The isolated occurrence of *desire* among these responses seems aberrant.

Two examples are given below in which *badly* is unacceptable. A detailed semantic and syntactic study of the two verbs is required before a full statement can be made of the use of the verbs that inhibit the acceptability of *badly* as a collocate.

(1) The Subject must not be impersonal *it, e.g.*:

He badly needs a good reason to make him do it.
*It badly needs a good reason to make him do it.

(2) For some informants the verb *want* must have an animate Subject, *e.g.*:

This room needs painting.
This room wants painting.
This room badly needs painting.
?*This room badly wants painting.

Before we leave our discussion of these two verbs, we should mention that some nouns recurred frequently in the Complement after *need*. The most frequent items were *drink* (20) and *money* (18). Other items appearing more than once after *need* were *rest* (14), *it* (8), *coat* (5), *haircut* (4), *pen* (3), *bath* (2), *wash* (2), *help* (2), and *holiday* (2). The only items to occur more than once after *want* were *drink* (4), *holiday* (2), and *it* (2).

Among the collocates for this test are some verbs that denote an action of injuring. With such verbs *badly* is a mixture of degree intensifier and manner adjunct. If we say *They wounded him badly* we are saying something about the extent of the wounding and at the same time referring to its unpleasant consequences, so that some of the literal meaning of *badly* is present.[8] *Badly* does not convey an unfavourable connotation when it is used as a pure degree intensifier, for example in *I badly need the money*. *Badly* may in fact collocate more frequently with verbs denoting injuring, such as *hurt* and *wound*, than the results of this test indicate. The explanation for the rarity of their appearance among the responses

---

[8] *Cf. They paid him badly* with its unfavourable implication 'paying too little'.

probably lies in the fact that *badly* collocates with them more normally when it is in post-verb position. When it is not a pure degree intensifier, pre-verb position is less acceptable.

There is some experimental evidence to support the argument that *badly* is fully acceptable in pre-verb position when it is a pure degree intensifier, unacceptable when it is a manner adjunct, and intermediate in the scale of acceptability between the two when it is a mixture of degree intensifier and manner adjunct. In the course of Battery IIIb the 70 informants were presented with three sentences containing *badly* in pre-verb position. The three sentences are given below with the task they were required to perform:

> he /badly needed the mòney#   [replacement of *he* by *they*]
> they /badly wounded the èlephant# [change of tense to present]
> they /badly treated the sèrvant#   [change of tense to present]

Badly in collocation with *needed* may be paraphrased by 'very much'; in collocation with *wounded* it may be paraphrased by a blend of 'greatly' and 'in a bad way' (closely paralleled by *severely* in collocation with *wounded*); in collocation with *treated* it may be paraphrased by 'in a bad way'. Table 17 displays the results for these three compliance tests. The columns from left to right list the number of compliant responses, the number of compliant responses without any overt signs of hesitation, and the number of transpositions of *badly* from pre-verb position. The results support the distinctions that have been made between the three types of *badly*.

TABLE 17

Compliance Tests with 'Badly'

	Compliances	Unhesitating compliances	Trans- positions
badly needed	70 (100)	68 (97)	0
badly wounded	54 (77)	40 (57)	15 (21)
badly treated	24 (34)	18 (26)	46 (66)

(BATTERY IIIb: 70 informants. Percentages are given in parentheses.)

The large number of hesitations that accompanied compliant responses for the sentence with *badly wounded* (14, 20 per cent, in contrast to only two for the first test, 3 per cent, and 6, 9 per cent, for the third test) indicates a great deal of vacillation over the sentence before it was written down compliantly. It should be mentioned that manner adjuncts are fully acceptable before the passive participle. All these three sentences are therefore acceptable:

The money was badly needed.
The elephant was badly wounded.
The servant was badly treated.

The three sentences with *badly* given in Battery IIIb were presented to informants in an earlier experiment, in the course of Battery IIIa. On that occasion they were asked to turn them into questions. The results are displayed in Table 18. We see from that Table that even when in collocation with *need, badly* is transposed from pre-verb position by most of the informants during the performance of the interrogative transformation. However, there still is greatest compliance for the sentence with *badly* in collocation with *need,* least for the sentence with *badly* in collocation with *treat,* while the sentence with *badly* and *wound* is intermediate in number of compliances. This gradience in acceptability is confirmed in the explicit evaluation tests, the results for which are displayed in Table 19. It is interesting that for the test with *badly* in collocation with *wound,* five informants transformed the sentence into the passive as well as making it a question, producing the responses *Was the elephant badly wounded?* (2), *Is the elephant badly wounded?* (2), and *Is this elephant badly wounded?* One informant incorporated the passive participle with *badly* as premodifier in a nominal group: *Is that a badly wounded elephant?* In this way the informants were able to retain badly before the verb acceptably.

TABLE 18

Compliance Tests with 'Badly': Interrogation

	Compliances	Unhesitating compliances	Trans-positions
badly needed	50 (43)	44 (38)	65 (56)
badly wounded	45 (38)	34 (29)	63 (54)
badly treated	27 (23)	25 (21)	89 (76)

(BATTERY IIIa: 117 informants. Percentages are given in parentheses.)

TABLE 19

Evaluation Tests with 'Badly'

	+	—	?
/did he badly need the móney#	58 (50)	25 (21)	34 (29)
/did they badly wound the sóldier#	48 (41)	34 (29)	35 (30)
/did they badly treat the sérvant#	16 (14)	53 (45)	48 (41)

(BATTERY IIIa: 117 informants. Percentages are given in parentheses.)

The choice of intensifier with some of the verbs of injuring may determine whether the verbs are interpreted as referring to physical or emotional injury. Thus, *They wounded him* may denote either physical wounding or emotional wounding. However, *They wounded him deeply* would be interpreted as emotional wounding, whereas *They wounded him badly* would be interpreted as physical wounding. *Deeply* as intensifier collocates with 'emotive verbs' (*cf.* Svartvik 1966, 84,148), such as *admire, provoke, insult, offend,* and it therefore selects the emotive sense of verbs like *wound, hurt,* and *upset.*[9]

Miscalculated and *misjudged* are rather like the collocates in the set of verbs of injuring in that *badly* in collocation with them is a blend of intensifier and manner adjunct. We may suppose that *badly* is in these cases in part reinforcing the sense of the

[9]   Svartvik points to the ability of some of these verbs to be premodified in the passive by *very* when they have the emotive sense. In, for example, the sentence *He was very wounded, wounded* would be interpreted in the emotive sense (Svartvik 1966, 148).

prefix *mis*. This explains why it is fairly acceptable in pre-verb position, as in the two responses:

I badly miscalculated the time allowed.
I badly misjudged him.

In collocation with *judge*, on the other hand, *badly* is only a manner adjunct. It seems far less acceptable in pre-verb position than when it is with *misjudge*:

*I badly judged the situation.

The few other collocates that occur seem to be aberrant, except for *fail*, with which *badly* is again a blend of intensifier and manner adjunct.

5.3   H4 *YOUR /FRIEND VERY MŪCH* : Ta3 *WE /ALL MŪCH* :
      Tb3 */SOME PEOPLE MŪCH*

Despite the differences between the principal collocates, the results of these three tests show some general resemblance. In the first place, the majority of the verbs in each of the tests denote an attitude either of the Subject towards the Complement or of the Complement towards the Subject. For example, in the sentence *Your friend very much dislikes me,* the referent of *your friend* is said to have an attitude of disliking towards the referent of *me*. On the other hand, in the sentence *Your friend very much impressed me*, the referent of the Complement *me* is said to have an attitude towards the referent of the Subject, *your friend*.[10] Table 20 demonstrates that a very large number of the responses for these three tests contain attitudinal verbs. Secondly, for all three tests the attitude denoted by most of the verbs is favourable. The proportion of unfavourable attitudes is lowest for the test with */some people mūch* with four items (*dislike* 3 and *hate* 1) or 6

[10] Verbs denoting the attitude of the Subject towards the Complement, such as *dislike* or *suspect* require an animate noun as Subject. On the other hand, verbs denoting the attitude of the Complement towards the Subject, such as *impress* or *amuse* require an animate noun as Complement.

per cent. For the test with *we /all much* there are nine items (*regret* 6, *fear* 1, *abhor* 1, *loathe* 1), 10 per cent, and for the test with *your /friend very much* there are 20 items (*dislike* 8, *regret* 7, *hate* 1, *suspect* 1, *doubt* 1, *irritate* 1, *annoy* 1), 19 per cent.

The two tests with *much* have three principal collocates each, two of which are the same for both tests, *admire* and *enjoy* (*cf.* Table 2, page 36). None of their principal collocates are principal collocates for the test with *your /friend very much*. There is some further evidence to link the two tests with *much* more closely to each other than either of them to the test with *very much*. The most frequent collocate for */some people much* is *prefer,* which appears 35 times (56 per cent). This verb occurs in the test with *we /all much*, though far less frequently (8 times, 9 per cent), but not at all in the test with *your /friend very much*. The absence of two of the principal collocates from the test with */some people much* is more understandable, since the total number of valid responses is rather small in this test. *Want*, a principal collocate for *your /friend very much*, appears only once with *we /all much* and it is not surprising that it should not appear at all in the responses for the smaller group if its frequency with *your /friend very much* is not because of the presence of *much* but because of the presence of the premodified group *very much*. One other principal collocate, *appreciate*, with a frequency of 9 (10 per cent) in the test with *we /all much* and the low frequency of 3 (2 per cent) in the test with *your /friend very much*, does not appear at all after */some people much*. Its absence in this last test may be ascribed to the influence of the Subject.

Since the differences between the two tests with *much* must be ascribed in part to differences between the Subjects of the two sentences,[11] we cannot be certain that the Subject of the test with *very much* has not influenced the choice of collocates. Nevertheless, the high frequency of *like* after *very much* and its relative infrequency after *much* in both tests suggests that premodification of *much* is an important factor in determining the collocates.

[11] The differences may be partly due to differences in the populations of the informants.

TABLE 20
Attitudinal Verbs

	S of Sentence = S of attitude	S of Sentence = 0 of attitude
BATTERY II		
H1 the /man cērtainly	10 (6%)	3 (5%)
H2 the /child rēally	39 (24%)	2 (1%)
H3 I /bādly	0	0
H4 your /friend very mūch	98 (61%)	6 (4%)
H5 they/all grēatly	160 (91%)	0
BATTERY IIIa		
Ta1 I en/tīrely	2 (2%)	0
Ta2 they /all ūtterly	36 (35%)	6 (6%)
Ta3 we /all mūch	78 (90%)	0
Ta4 my /friend complētely	21 (18%)	6 (5%)
BATTERY IIIb		
Tb1 my /friend entīrely	9 (13%)	1 (1%)
Tb2 his /father ūtterly	33 (48%)	3 (4%)
Tb3 /some people mūch	63 (100%)	0
Tb4 I com/plētely	6 (9%)	1 (1%)

Further evidence is afforded by the frequency of *want* after *very much* as compared with the one instance after *we /all mūch* and its absence after */some people mūch*. We have earlier referred to the difference between *much* and *very much* when they are in post-verb position in affirmative sentences, *cf.* page 12.[12]

[12] It is of interest to compare the results of the completion tests on *much* and *very much* with the findings of Behre (1967, 73 ff., 175 ff.). As fas as I can ascertain, Behre records 25 occurrences of *much* in pre-verb position and 30 occurrences of *very much* in the same position. In some instances the intensifier is between the auxiliary and the lexical verb, but Behre does not always distinguish these instances, which might have a bearing on the collocation, from instances when there is no auxiliary present. If we ignore this distinction, we find the following verbs collocating with *much* and *very much* in his corpus, when the intensifiers are in pre-verb position:

very much: doubt 9, *wonder* 8, *like* 4, *fear* 4, *wish* 3, *hope* 1, *prefer* 1
much: prefer 10, *appreciate* 5, *like* 3, *regret* 3, *fear* 3, *enjoy* 1

All the collocates in this corpus for *very much* occur in the completion test after *your /friend very mūch* except for *fear* and *prefer*. However, *want*, a principal collocate in the completion test, does not appear in the

Two verbs that appear among the collocates of *your /friend very much* collocate with *very much* in only one of the senses of the verbs. *Miss* in its emotive sense of 'feel sorry or unhappy at the loss or absence of' collocates with this degree intensifier. In its various senses of failing or omitting, *miss* does not collocate with *very much*. Thus, *They missed the bus* would not allow the addition of *very much* in the normal interpretation of the sentence, 'They failed to catch the bus'. *They missed her* would allow both the interpretation 'They felt unhappy that she was absent', in which case *very much* is admissible, and the interpretation "They failed to meet her', in which case *very much* is inadmissible. Similarly, *appeal* collocates with *very much* only when the verb has the emotive sense of 'arouse a favourable feeling'. Thus, the response in the completion test, *Your friend very much appeals to me*, presumably represents the emotive sense of *appeals*. On the other hand, if we were to inhibit the emotive sense by adding *for help* to this sentence, the incorporation of the degree intensifier would produce an unacceptable sentence:

*Your friend *very much* appeals to me for help.
*Your friend appeals to me for help *very much*.[13]

The verb *thank* collocates with *very much* (and *much* plus other premodifiers, such as *so* or *too*). However, *very much* seems to be restricted to post-verb position in this collocation. The response

---

corpus, and the frequency of *like* in the completion test is not reflected in the corpus, though it should be added that *like* and *very much* collocate frequently when the intensifier is in post-verb position. All the collocates for *much* in the corpus appear in the completion test after *we /all much*, but three verbs (*appreciate, regret,* and *fear*) are absent after /*some people much*. The high frequency of *prefer* corresponds to what we find in the test with /*some people much*. On the other hand, *admire*, which is a principal collocate in both tests with *much* is absent from the corpus. We may assume that there must be some skewing of the results of the corpus in view of the very small numbers involved. It should be added that some of the collocates may represent an attempt to reproduce the unidiomatic speech of foreign speakers of English (*cf.* Behre 1967, 124).

[13] *Cf.* the restriction of *deeply* as degree intensifier to emotive senses of certain verbs, page 66.

by one informant of *Your friend very much thanked me* is therefore rather odd. This positional restriction may be caused by the
influence of the frequent collocations *Thanks very much* and
Thank you very much, in which *very much* is always after *thanks*
or *thank*. The wish for emphasis on the degree intensifier in these
conventional expressions may have determined the placement in
final position.[14]

Among the miscellaneous collocates at least one seems aberrant: *Your friend very much has writer's cramp*. It is presumably
a facetious comment by the informant on his own condition.

Another response *Your friend very much would like to come*
is an exception to the general rule that degree intensifiers cannot
precede auxiliaries (*cf.* above, page 27). However, *would like* is a
special case, since semantically *would* is part of a lexical unit
equivalent to *want* or *wish* and is not merely the modal auxiliary.
(This applies also to *should like* if used as a variant of *would like*
with the first person.)

5.4   H5 *THEY/ALL GRĒATLY*

Almost all the verbs that collocate with *they /all grēatly* are
attitudinal and express an attitude of the Subject towards the
referent of the Complement, *cf.* Table 20. There is a considerable
resemblance between the range of verbs that collocate with *they
/all grēatly* and those that collocate with the sentence openings
containing *much* or *very much*. In particular, the tests with *greatly*
and *much* have in common *admire* and *enjoy* as principal collocates. What distinguishes the test with *greatly* from the others is
the high frequency of *admire*, which appears in 44 per cent of the
responses (*cf.* Table 2, page 36).

As with *very much, greatly* only collocates with *miss* in its

---

[14]   "A tone group is neutral in tonicity if the tonic falls on the last ele-
ment of grammatical structure that contains a lexical item." (Halliday
1963, 18).

emotive sense. The five instances of *applaud* are interesting, since this verb may denote merely approval or it may signify a physical act expressing approval. In one response the Complement *his manners* virtually excludes the physical sense of *applaud*. The others allow both senses: *his act, his display, his performance,* and *the actors*. However, the theatrical context that is implied strongly suggests the physical sense of *applaud*. The attitudinal sense that is always present in *applaud* has presumably allowed its collocation with *greatly* even when the physical sense is also present. The verb *worship* is an analogous case. A physical sense is presumably implied in the response with *the sun* as Complement, since *worship* probably indicates an act of worshipping, but the attitudinal sense of regarding with respect or devotion is also present.

The two verbs of activity, *fight* and *overdrink,* seem to be aberrant in collocation with *greatly*.

5.5   Ta1 *I EN/TĪRELY* : Tb1 *MY/FRIEND ENTĪRELY*

The most frequent collocate after *I en/tīrely* is *agree*. Its frequency rate of 82 per cent represents the highest for any collocate in the completion tests. The drop in the frequency rate after *my /friend entīrely* to 56 per cent demonstrates the influence of the Subject of the sentence in determining the selection of the verb. Nevertheless, the influence of the intensifier is clearly paramount. We can contrast the frequency rate of 56 per cent for *agree* after *my /friend entīrely* with its frequency rate of 3 per cent after *my /friend complētely*. Since the Subject is constant in both these tests, we can only ascribe the high frequency of *agree* in one of the tests to the intensifier *entirely*. Similarly, we may contrast the very high frequency of 82 per cent for *agree* after *I en/tīrely* with its complete absence after *I /bādly* and its low frequency of 7 per cent after *I com/plētely*. Again, it is obvious that it is the intensifier *entirely* rather than the Subject *I* that is determining the collocation with *agree*. The presence of the Subject has a bearing

on the frequency of *agree* as a collocate of *entirely,* but in both
tests it is the most frequent collocate.

In both tests the next most frequent collocate (and the only
verb to appear more than twice) is *disagree,* the antonym of *agree.*
Other verbs that are common to both tests are *forget, believe,* and
give oneself. Two of the verbs after *my /friend entirely* seem
aberrant collocates of *entirely,* at least when it is in pre-verb position. The two verbs are *eat* and *tell,* and they appear in the responses *My friend entirely ate the cake* and *My friend entirely
told the truth.* It is significant that these are verbs of activity. The
verb *left* appears in the meaning 'abandon' in one response: *My
friend entirely left it to me.* If the physical sense of *left* is required,
its collocation with *entirely* in pre-verb position is unacceptable:
*My friend entirely left Waterloo Station.

5.6 Ta2 *THEY /ALL ŪTTERLY* : Tb2 *HIS /FATHER ŪTTERLY*

The low percentages of the two principal collocates after these
tests, *hate* and *despise,* with frequency rates of 10 per cent, suggests that there is not a strong collocational tie between *utterly*
and any particular verb (*cf.* Table 2, page 36). On the other hand,
almost all the verbs have some 'negative' implication, suggesting
disapproval, opposition, or failure.[15] There is therefore a collocational tie with a semantically identifiable class of verbs. A similar
range of verbs with 'negative' import is found in the tests with

---

[15]   This has been pointed out by others. For example, OED notes at the
head of one of its sections in its entry for *utterly* that it is frequently 'with
verbs of perishing, refusal, etc.'. At the head of the section on *utterly* as
a qualifier of adjectives OED has the parenthesis: '(freq. from 1660, esp.
with words implying negation, defeat, or opposition)'. Borst (1902, 123)
notes the predilection of *utterly* to associate with negative concepts ('wird
im Ne. mit Verliebe mit negativen Begriffen verbunden') and instances a
number of verbs that associate with it: *to forget, to extinguish, to despise,
to deny, to forsake.* Zimmer (1964, 89) draws attention in a note to the
fact that '*utterly* seems to be used with "negative" rather than with "posi-
tive" adjectives'.

completely, but with these tests there are one or two verbs that occur very frequently.

The 'negativeness' of most of the verbs that occur in the tests with *utterly* and *completely* contrasts with the 'positiveness' of most of the verbs that appear in the tests with *very much* and *much* (cf. pages 67 ff.) and with *they /all grēatly* (cf. pages 71 f.). We must ascribe this difference to the degree intensifier rather than to the Subject, since one of the tests with *utterly* has the same Subject as the test with *greatly*. The 'negativeness' of the verbs that collocate with *utterly* is underlined by the prevalence among them of prefixes or 'prefixoids' that have a 'negative' feeling about them.[16] Table 21 lists the frequency of the prefixes or 'prefixoids' *dis-, des-,* and *de-* for all the tests in the Battery. The much higher proportion of these for the two tests with *utterly* is evident.

Utterly collocates with the verbs *stink* and *revolt* only in their emotive sense. Whereas *stink* in collocation with *certainly* may refer to the emission of an unpleasant smell, in collocation with *utterly* it means 'to arouse loathing'. *Revolt* has a similar meaning in collocation with *utterly,* though it differs from *stink* in being transitive. In the sense of 'rebel', *revolt* does not collocate with *utterly*. The sentence **The tribe utterly revolted against their chief* would therefore be deviant.

Several of the responses seem unacceptable: *They all utterly enjoyed the concert, They all utterly cried out, They all utterly killed themselves laughing,* and *They all utterly had a marvellous time*. The collocation of *utterly* and *kill* in the physical sense seems rather odd in the response *His father utterly killed him,* since the verb *kill* is not gradable. We must assume that for this informant *utterly* has an intensifying force only and does not signify an extreme degree.

Several verbs that appear in the tests with *utterly* do not have a 'negative' import and yet do not seem unacceptable collocates.

---

[16] 'Prefixoids' are sound sequences that resemble genuine prefixes without qualifying for that rank (*cf.* Malkiel 1966, 322-3).

The verb *agree* occurs a number of times in both tests and the verbs *trust* and *depend upon* appear once after *his /father ütterly*. It is possible that the latter two verbs have some 'negative' import when they collocate with *utterly,* an implication that trusting to such an extent is a defect. If such an implication is indeed present, it could be explained as a result of the habitual collocation of *utterly* with 'negative' verbs.

It should be mentioned here that *utterly* is the only one of the degree intensifiers that for many native speakers of English cannot occupy a position after the verb (*cf.* pages 31, 50). The results for the tests with *utterly* may therefore have a more general significance for statements about the collocations of verbs with *utterly,* since for the other results we must add the rider that they only tell us about the collocates of the intensifiers in pre-verb position.

TABLE 21

Verb Prefixes and Prefixoids 'Dis', 'Des', and 'De'

	Total valid responses	DIS	DES	DE	Combined total
BATTERY II					
H1 the /man cērtainly	173	1 (1%)		3 (2%)	4 (2%)
H2 the /child rēally	165				0 (0%)
H3 I /bādly	175			1 (1%)	1 (1%)
H4 your /friend very mūch	161	8 (5%)			8 (5%)
H5 they /all grēatly	176	2 (1%)	2 (1%)	2 (1%)	6 (3%)
BATTERY IIIa					
Ta1 I en/tīrely	108	11 (10%)			11 (10%)
Ta2 they /all ütterly	103	21 (20%)	10 (10%)	11 (10%)	42 (41%)
Ta3 we /all mūch	87			5 (6%)	5 (6%)
Ta4 my /friend complētely	117	6 (5%)		6 (5%)	12 (10%)
BATTERY IIIb					
Tb1 my /friend entīrely	68	8 (12%)		1 (1%)	9 (13%)
Tb2 his /father ütterly	69	10 (14%)	8 (12%)	8 (12%)	26 (38%)
Tb3 /some people mūch	63	3 (5%)		1 (2%)	4 (6%)
Tb4 I com/plētely	70	4 (6%)	1 (1%)		5 (7%)

5.7   Ta4 *MY /FRIEND COMPLĒTELY* : Tb4 *I COM/PLĒTELY*

In both these tests the most frequent collocate is *forget*. It is reasonable to assume that *forget* collocates with the degree intensifier *completely* rather than with the Subject. First, *forget* is the most frequent collocate whether the Subject is *my friend* or *I*. Secondly, we find no instances of *forget* after *I /bādly* and only one instance of *forget* after *I en/tīrely* and *my /friend entīrely*. The only other principal collocate, *ignore*, is principal collocate only after *my /friend complētely*. The infrequency of its appearance after *I com/plētely* must therefore be ascribed to the inhibiting influence of the changed Subject or to the absence of the interacting stimulus of *my friend* and *entirely*.[17]

We have seen that the tests with *utterly* and *completely* have in common a large majority of verbs with 'negative' import. There are, however, some differences between the semantic groupings that occur after these intensifiers. First, there are many more verbs denoting a failure to attain a desirable goal or state after *completely* than there are after *utterly*. And secondly, there are a number of verbs of disliking after *utterly* and hardly any after *completely*.[18]

The collocates after *my /friend complētely* include a small group of verbs of surprising. It is interesting that Klima (1964, 311 ff.) has shown that these verbs, as well as some others that occur as collocates of *completely* and *utterly* (viz. *deny, forget, refuse*), share a syntactic feature with negatives. They permit indefinite quantifiers in the Complement clause. Thus, we may have sentences such as *It surprises me that he has any money* or *He was astonished that she ever speaks to them*. He terms these verbs (and other words allowing indefinite quantifiers in Complement

---

[17]   It is interesting that *forget* and *ignore* share a common semantic feature of neglecting, but whereas *forget* usually denotes accidental or unintentional neglecting, *ignore* denotes wilful neglecting. Webster's Third New International Dictionary cites *neglect* as a synonym of both these verbs.

[18]   With some verbs collocating with *utterly (disgust, revolt,* and *stink),* the referent of the Subject arouses dislike, *cf.* pages 69 (Table 20), 74.

TABLE 22

Attitudinal Meaning of Sentence with Respect to Subject

	Total valid responses	Compli- mentary to Subject of Sentence	Dispar- aging to Subject of Sentence	Neutral to Subject of Sentence
BATTERY II				
H1 the /man cērtainly	173	50 (29%)	41 (24%)	82 (47%)
H2 the /child rēally	165	23 (14%)	59 (36%)	83 (50%)
H3 I /bādly	175		12 (7%)	163 (93%)
H4 your /friend very mūch	161	3 (2%)	6 (4%)	152 (94%)
H5 they /all grēatly	176	1 (1%)		176 (99%)
BATTERY IIIa				
Ta1 I en/tīrely	108			108 (100%)
Ta2 they /all ūtterly	103		18 (18%)	85 (83%)
Ta3 we /all mūch	87			87 (100%)
Ta4 my /friend complētely	117	2 (2%)	69 (59%)	46 (39%)
BATTERY IIIb				
Tb1 my /friend entīrely	68	1 (1%)	5 (7%)	62 (91%)
Tb2 his /father ūtterly	69		15 (22%)	54 (78%)
Tb3 /some people mūch	63		1 (2%)	62 (98%)
Tb4 I com/plētely	70	1 (1%)	44 (63%)	25 (36%)

clauses) 'Adversatives' and ascribes to them 'a common gram-
matico-semantic feature to be referred to as *Affect*(ive)'.

The sentences with *completely* mostly express a disparagement
of the Subject of the sentence, as we can see from Table 22. Such
an attitude to the Subject necessarily follows from the high proportion of verbs that denote failing in some way. Table 22 shows
that a disparaging attitude to the Subject is expressed more frequently with this intensifier (even when the Subject is *I*) than with
any other intensifer.

Several of the responses seem odd when *completely* is in pre-
verb position. In some cases this is perhaps because the degree
import of *completely* is paramount and it affects the Complement. Thus, *completely runs my life* can be paraphrased by 'runs
the whole of my life', *completely dissected the animal* by 'dissected
all of the animal', *completely shared the flat* by 'shared all of
the flat', and *completely finished the book* by 'finished the whole
of the book'. We might cite as a contrast *completely forgot our
appointment,* which cannot be paraphrased by 'forgot the whole
of our appointment'. In two responses *completely* seems rather
odd in pre-verb position, even though the sentences cannot be
paraphrased in this way: *completely fell in love* and *completely
lost her way.*[19]

---

[19]   *Cf.* the compliance and evaluation tests in respect to the position of
completely in collocation with *manage*, a synonym for *runs* in the response
runs my life (pages 50 ff.).

6

CONCLUSIONS

6.1 TEST TECHNIQUE

The experiments that have been described in this study indicate that the type of operational test I have termed 'completion test' can supply useful information about collocations and their frequencies. They also suggest the possibility in some cases of extrapolating from the data to establish semantic sets of lexical items that can collocate in a particular syntactic relationship with a given item or set of items.

The responses to completion tests constitute a body of strictly comparable material, thereby greatly facilitating the study of collocations. It has been shown above (pages 36 ff.) that while there may be a restricted range of verbs available as collocates of a particular intensifier, other items in the sentence also influence the selection of verbs. The control that completion tests provide over such variables is a particular advantage that they have over the analysis of collocations in a corpus. This advantage is some compensation for the artificiality of the task, which requires the completion of sentences outside a linguistic context.[1] We can also point to the ease of collection of data on specific points. A corpus

[1] Informants may relate the sentence to the situational context, particularly when the Subject that they have been given is in the first person. This is certainly true of such completions after *I /bādly* as 'want to get out of here and stop mucking about', 'want this recording to stop', and 'wonder why words are repeated'. It is probably also true of 'want to stop writing so fast', 'want to leave as time is late', 'want to go home', 'need a rest', among many others. A striking example is a reference by name to the person conducting the experiment: 'We all much admire you, Professor Quirk.'

would have to be immense indeed to yield similar numbers of examples.[2]

It is relevant to mention at this point that we can reduce the effect of the Subject's influence on the selection of verbs following the intensifier by restricting the Subject to a pronoun. Even so, we must still take into account the possibility that different pronouns may evoke different verbs. For example, it seems unlikely that *agree* would be a frequent collocate of *You entirely*, though it appeared in 82 per cent of the responses after *I entirely*.

If an investigation into collocations is based solely on information derived from introspection, its reliability may be impugned on two grounds. In the first place, we would be justified in suspecting that the investigator has failed to recall some frequent collocations. And secondly, we can place no confidence in his ability to remember the relative frequency of collocations he has used or heard.

The completion tests discussed in this study did not allow for the variability in collocations and in the frequency of collocations that might emerge from a discrimination between varieties of the language. It would be possible to introduce more linguistic context and even an indication of the hypothetical situational context into

---

[2]   It is instructive to refer to the material that Behre has collected from a corpus of 4,200,000 words, *cf.* above, page 69, note 12. Behre records 340 occurrences of *much* or *very much* that appear in his corpus in the patterns Noun + Verb + *(very) much* or Noun + *(very) much* + Verb. Of these 17 are quantifiers or frequentatives, which we may exclude on two grounds: we are considering the use of these items only as intensifiers, and we are concerned only with the pre-verb position, which the quantifiers and frequentatives do not occupy. That leaves 323 instances, these being distributed between Subject and verb, between auxiliary and verb, and in some position after the verb. Behre does not always make it clear where the intensifier is positioned, but as far as I can ascertain he records 25 instances of *much* and 30 instances of *very much* in pre-verb position. If we ignore the fact that some of these are certainly positioned after the auxiliary, it remains that there is considerably less material for *much* and *very much* in pre-verb position in this corpus of over four million words than there is in the experimental data. We have for the completion tests 161 responses for the test with *very much* and a total of 150 responses for the two tests with *much*.

future experiments, though in practice it would be easier to do so if the material is presented visually (see below). Nevertheless, because of the overriding effect of the experimental situation, the results are unlikely to be representative of a particular variety of the language. It would, however, be interesting to correlate the results of such experiments with the results of corpus studies on corresponding varieties.

For collocations with high frequencies in completion tests, corpus studies can usefully establish their relative frequency in different varieties of the language, though probably for most collocations an extremely large corpus (of a size impossible to determine *a priori*) would be necessary. In the stylistic analysis of literary works, a study of collocations may reveal the predilection of individual writers or genres for particular collocations, their avoidance of collocations that are frequent elsewhere, and their selection of collocations that are rare or unique.

6.1.1 *Other Forms of the Completion Test*

In the experiments that have been conducted so far, the opening words of the completion tests were given orally whereas the informants produced their sentences in writing. It is possible that there may be some differences in the range or frequency of collocates if both the stimulus and the response are in the same medium. To test whether the medium is a significant variable, two experiments are necessary. In the first, the opening words of the completion tests are given visually, either on a slide or in a duplicated booklet, and the informants write down the sentences. In the second, the opening words are given orally and the informants respond orally. The results of these two experiments can then be compared with the results that are reported here.

Other forms of the completion test may be employed to supply information on similar problems of collocation. Some examples are given:

(1) Informants may be asked to complete a sentence ending with a given word.

(2) Informants may be given one or more words and may then be asked to provide a beginning and end to the sentence. If the material is provided in visual form, on a slide or in a duplicated booklet, the instruction could be 'Fill the missing spaces on either side of the word(s)'.

(3) If information on positional restrictions or positional preferences is desired, informants could be given the instruction: 'Use the word(s) *X (YZ)* with this sentence'. In this way it would be possible to investigate whether a particular item tended to be placed differently in collocation with different items.[3]

(4) We may wish to give the sentences and require information on what word is selected most often to fill a given space. For example, if we wish to find out the pre-verb intensifiers that occur most frequently with a particular verb, we could give the instruction: 'Fill the missing space in the sentence with one word'. To prevent insertions that might be irrelevant for our purposes, we could provide the *-ly* suffix in the sentence, *e.g.* 'They . . . ly need some money'. While this formulation would exclude, for example, *perhaps* and *often*, it would nevertheless permit *frequently* and *unfortunately* among other insertions irrelevant to the purpose of the test.

(5) A more restrictive requirement would be entailed by an instruction to fill a missing space with a word having a specified meaning. For example, informants could be asked to fill the missing space in the sentence *They . . . need some money* with a word meaning 'very much'.

In a further experiment informants might be required to complete a sentence a specified number of times. With the type of tests that have been described we might find that the same verbs are repeated after some of the opening words. On the other hand, we might find that by the fourth or fifth time deviant collocations abound because of the informants' wish to vary the verbs.

---

[3] Formulas such as 'Include the word(s) in the sentence' or 'Add the word(s) to the sentence' may suggest positions to informants and therefore skew results. In the first formulation it may predispose them to eschew the beginning or end of the sentence, and in the second, to choose these positions.

6.2 VERB-INTENSIFIER COLLOCATIONS

Statements of the range of verbs that collocate with particular pre-verb intensifiers will be different in kind. For some intensifiers, *e.g. utterly,* the collocational range of verbs can be defined semantically. For others, there appears to be a collocational range of verbs that are semantically homogeneous, but nevertheless some verbs that are apparently in the same semantic group are unacceptable as collocates. For example, *deeply* collocates with (among other verbs) *hate, dislike, admire, love,* and *value,* yet **deeply like* is an unacceptable collocation, though *like* collocates with *very much,* as do these other verbs. In such a case, while we can generalise in semantic terms on the collocational range of verbs, we must also list exceptions to our generalisations. Finally, for some intensifiers, *e.g. badly,* all we can do is specify the individual verbs with which they may collocate.

In the Appendix, *ad hoc* semantic groups have been listed for the responses to each test. Some semantic features cutting across these divisions have been noted earlier: (i) many of the verbs collocating with the degree intensifiers *(very) much, greatly,* and *utterly are* attitudinal *(cf.* Table 20, page 69); (ii) most of the attitudinal verbs collocating with *(very) much* and *greatly* express a favourable attitude, while those collocating with *utterly* express an unfavourable attitude (pages 71, 73); (iii) most of the verbs collocating with *utterly* and *completely* have a negative implication, suggesting disapproval, opposition, or failure (pages 73, 76); (iv) most of the sentences with *completely* express a disparagement of the Subject of the sentence (pages 77 f.).

We have also noted that verbs of activity are virtually absent from the collocates of the degree intensifiers, though they appear with some frequency among the collocates of *certainly* and *really* (page 57). The verbs of activity that are acceptable collocates of degree intensifiers comprise the few instances of verbs of destruction that collocate with *utterly.* Apart from these exceptions, it seems that verbs of activity do not collocate with degree intensifiers. On the other hand, it seems that manner adjuncts do not collocate with most of the verb collocates of degree intensifiers, including in particular attitudinal verbs. Although further investigation is necessary, it appears that manner adjuncts are restricted to collocation with verbs of activity. Several instances have been given to show that where a verb has more than one sense the non-activity sense is selected when the verb is in collocation with a degree intensifier (pages 66, 70, 71 f., 73, 74). Similarly, in such a case the activity sense is selected when the verb is in collocation with a manner adjunct. A recent London newspaper headline read *Mr Smith appeals to Mr Wilson*. Outside the situational and linguistic context, this sentence is ambiguous. It may be paraphrased either by 'Mr Smith makes an urgent request to Mr Wilson' or by 'Mr Smith has qualities that are attractive to Mr Wilson'. The addition of a manner adjunct disambiguates the sentence in favour of the first paraphrase, *e.g. Mr Smith appeals to Mr Wilson courteously,* while the addition of a degree intensifier disambiguates it in favour of the second paraphrase, *e.g. Mr Smith greatly appeals to Mr Wilson*. Collocability with either degree intensifiers or manner adjuncts or both distinguishes between classes of verbs.

Statements are also required of the strength of the collocational link between an intensifier and particular verbs. Thus, *badly* has been shown to collocate very frequently with *need* and frequently with *want*, while *entirely* collocates very frequently with *agree*. On the other hand, *utterly* does not appear to have a strong collocational link with particular verbs.

For a study of collocations that will result in rules that can be incorporated in a generative grammar, it is necessary to distinguish between the possible (even if never used) collocations and those that violate syntactic, lexical, or semantic rules. As so often in language, we can expect to find a scale of acceptability rather than a clear demarcation between the acceptable and the unacceptable. The evaluation and compliance tests (*cf.* pages 50 ff.) will provide evidence of the degree of acceptability of collocations.

However, it is also linguistically relevant to determine which are the strong collocational links in the language. The occasional collocation may imply, through one of the items, an analogy with the habitual collocation. An example is given from outside the area we have been investigating. The word *delinquency* habitually collocates with a premodifying adjective *juvenile*. Recently, the collocations *midde-aged delinquency* and *senile delinquency* have been used in British newspapers. These are interpreted not merely to denote misbehaviour practised by the middle-aged and the senile respectively, but also to imply that it resembles a form associated with young people. The frequency of the collocation *juvenile delinquency* is relevant to a synchronic statement of the meaning of the other two collocations.

The premodifiers *middle-aged* and *senile* share with *juvenile* a reference to a period in the life of a human being. We can project new formations along these lines that would presumably be acceptable and would be interpreted in the same way, for example, *infant delinquency*. The fewer the semantic features the premodifier of the newly-created collocation has in common with *juvenile*, the more the collocation will be felt to depart from everyday language. Thus, we might arrange a gradient of similarity to *juvenile* of four premodifiers:

juvenile	+animate	+human	+age-range	+age (?)10-16
middle-aged	+animate	+human	+age-range	
secretarial	+animate	+human		
feline	+animate			
metal				

A poet might ascribe the fault for an airplane disaster to *metal delinquency*. In doing so, he would be attributing to the metal the irresponsibility typical of the juvenile delinquent. Such a coinage would receive reinforcement by its echo of the collocation *metal fatigue,* which is no longer felt to be a living metaphor. The hypothetical coinage of *metal delinquency* is an example of the 'linguistic audacity' found in poetry (*cf.* Leech 1968, 29 ff.).

Let us now turn to the intensifiers for an anecdotal instance of the relevance of strong collocational links. We have earlier noticed the negative import of the collocates of *utterly* (page 73 f.). At a meeting of a University Department, a new degree course was being devised. One lecturer, who was opposed to the abandonment of the existing syllabus, raised the question: 'Are we utterly free to devise our own syllabus?' The use of *utterly* as premodifier of *free*, a word that normally has favourable connotations, turned *free* into a pejorative, consonant with the lecturer's view in this context.

From his experience of the language, the native speaker of English becomes aware whether a collocation he produces or encounters is habitual or occasional or unique and deviating from everyday language. The non-native speaker needs to learn in the first place the habitual collocations. Information about which degree intensifiers collocate with which verbs is of some importance to the foreign learner. He may easily come to form aberrant collocations by limiting himself to one degree intensifier, perhaps *much,* with or without the premodifier *very.* Behre notes that in Agatha Christie's writings, *much* is frequently used in dialogue by foreign characters, 'who anxiously stick to it' (Behre 1967, 124). It may be supposed that Agatha Christie is imitating the unidiomatic use of *much* by foreign speakers of English.

The collocational link between pre-verb intensifiers and verbs has been determined in the completion tests by the presence of the pre-verb intensifiers. However, it is reasonable to assume that in practice the speaker or writer selects the verb first and the pre-verb intensifier afterwards or perhaps both as a unit. I make this assumption for two reasons: (1) the verb is obligatory in the syntactic structure of the sentence while the intensifier is optional and can therefore be omitted, and (2) one would expect the selection of an intensifier to follow the decision to select the word to be intensified. Nevertheless, it seems advisable to state the collocational range from the point of view of the intensifier. There are far fewer intensifiers than verbs in the language. Consequently, it is more economical to mark each intensifier with a range of verbs than to mark each verb with a range of intensifiers.

How can we incorporate into a description of English the collocational restrictions and collocational frequencies that have been defined in this study? Neither semantic rules nor syntactic rules nor a combination of these seem capable of handling the restrictions on collocation, let alone the frequencies of collocation. It would appear that this information is best stored in the lexicon. The lexicon should contain for each degree intensifier a specification of the collocational range of verbs and refer to individual verbs that have a strong collocational link. In some cases, e.g. *utterly*, all that is necessary is to specify the semantic features of the groups of verbs (and in the lexicon these features are to be noted for the individual verbs);[4] in other cases, e.g. *deeply*, we need, in addition to such generalisations, to list individual exceptions, verbs that do not collocate with the intensifier though they possess the specified semantic features; and there will also be cases, e.g. *badly*, where individual verbs must be listed, since no generalisations can be made. The strength of the collocational link can be expressed on the basis of the results of completion tests. One approach would be to grade the percentages arbitrarily, so that, for example, 20%-39% is termed '*D*-strength' and 80%-100% is termed '*A*-strength'. Alternatively, the percentages themselves might be given.[5] Together with these specifications, the lexicon must also state the positional and other syntactic restrictions on collocations that are otherwise acceptable (*cf.* page 12).

[4] The semantic features may be identical to those for adjective and adverb collocates of the intensifier and this information would also be stated. See the remarks quoted on page 73, note 15, on the adjective collocates of *utterly*.

[5] Since writing this I have seen that Bolinger (1969, 37 f.) has proposed the indication of percentage probabilities in the lexicon for certain grammatical information.

APPENDIX: SEMANTIC GROUPING OF COLLOCATES

H1 *the /man cĕrtainly*

PERSONAL ATTRIBUTES:
  (i) INTELLECTUAL: be a fool (6); not be a fool; be foolish; not
  be very bright; be very intelligent; be clever; not be very
  clever; be stupid; be crackers; be insane
  TOTAL: 15 (9%)
  (ii) PHYSICAL: be drunk (2); not be good-looking; look attractive;
  look well; look ill; look peaky; look odd; look all right; look
  nice; look stupid; look tired; look like a tramp; have a bald
  head; dress well (2); be well-dressed; be unsteady on feet; be
  tall (2); be strong; smell; stink
  TOTAL: 23 (13%)
  (iii) PSYCHOLOGICAL, MORAL, EMOTIVE, STATUS, ETC.: look happy;
  be guilty; be a fraud; be tricky; not be very adamant; be a
  bore; be a V.I.P.; be dignified; be weird; be brave; be honest;
  be sex-starved; be unfortunate; be good at football
  TOTAL: 14 (8%)
TOTAL: 52 (30%)

INTELLECTUAL STATE: know (22); not know (4); think; not understand; not believe
TOTAL: 29 (17%)

LIKING & DISLIKING: like (4); not like; dislike; love; hate (2)
TOTAL: 9 (5%)

MOVEMENT: run (7); walk (2); go (4); not go (2); not come; not
arrive; drive; dance; can-can; swim; fall; not be going to fall
in; fall off; not get very far
TOTAL 25 (14%)

OTHER VERBS OF ACTIVITY: eat (2); not eat; drink (3); smoke; snore; yell; speak; say; make point; lie; read; write; play; hit; fight (2); not kill; work (3); not work (2); wash face; never do the deed; do well (2); do job well; do it; not do it (2)
TOTAL: 33 (19%)

MISCELLANEOUS: be here; be there; be; enjoy self; win; terrify; get own way; carry conviction; react predictably; miss opportunity; have a raw deal; lose money; fall for it; wear a hat; not stay; be surprised; astound; show self up; get what he deserved; have a lot to do; have lots to do; do; do not; deserve (2)
TOTAL: 25 (14%)

H2   *the /child rēally*

PERSONAL ATTRIBUTES:

(i) INTELLECTUAL: be a genius; be clever (2); be intelligent (2); be a fool; be a simpleton; be stupid (2); be backward (2); be mad
TOTAL: 12 (7%)

(ii) PHYSICAL; be good-looking; be pretty; be ugly; look well; look ill (4); be healthy; smell
TOTAL: 10 (6%)

(iii) PSYCHOLOGICAL, MORAL, EMOTIVE, STATUS, ETC.: be mischievous; be a lively one; be naughty (6); be a nuisance (3); be annoying; be well-behaved (2); be better-behaved; be bad; be good (2); not be good; be spoilt (3); be immature; be a horror; be funny; be a comedian; be unhappy; be brave; be abnormal; be just like his mother; come from a rich family; go to a good school
TOTAL: 32 (19)

TOTAL: 54 (33%)

INTELLECTUAL STATE: know; not know (7); not understand (4); think hard; imagine; have no idea; believe (3)
TOTAL: 18 (11%)

LIKING & DISLIKING: love (16); hate (7); like (6); adore; lap it up
TOTAL: 31 (19%)

CRYING: cry (6); not cry; scream; howl; yell
TOTAL: 10 (6%)
OTHER VERBS OF ACTIVITY: do it; not do well; not work; eat (3); write; ask; not read; run away; go home; go to school; go to tea
TOTAL: 13 (8%)
MISCELLANEOUS: need (5); want (4); be tired; be upset; be in a temper; not be allowed to do it (2); not try; try (2); care; not care (2); give of best; impress; not help it; enjoy (4); enjoy self; hurt self (2); stop eating; have a toothache; feel ill; grow (2); stay; lose way; fall out of; ought to be in bed
TOTAL: 39 (24%)

H3   *I /bădly*

NEEDING & WANTING: need (113); want (49); desire
TOTAL: 163 (93%)
INJURING: hurt; hurt self; injure; sprain; pain
TOTAL: 5 (3%)
JUDGING: judge; misjudge; miscalculate
TOTAL: 3 (2%)
MISCELLANEOUS: fail; wonder; attempt; refuse
TOTAL: 4 (2%)

H4   *your /friend very mŭch*

LIKING & DISLIKING: like (46); love (3); fancy the idea of; dislike (8); hate
TOTAL: 59 (37%)
NEEDING & WANTING: need (12); lack; want (29); wish (6); desire
TOTAL: 49 (30%)
OTHER ATTITUDINAL VERBS: admire (10); appreciate (3); regret (7); miss (6); hope (4); enjoy (7); appeal; suspect; doubt; impress (2); irritate; annoy; interest; amuse
TOTAL: 46 (29%)
MISCELLANEOUS: thank; remind; resemble; look like; agree; wonder; have writer's cramp
TOTAL: 7 (4%)

H5   *they /all grēatly*

LIKING & DISLIKING: like (4); love (6); fall in love with; adore; dislike (2); hate (3)

TOTAL: 17 (10%)

WANTING & NEEDING: want (4); wish (2); desire; need (2)

TOTAL: 9 (5%)

ADMIRING: admire (78); worship him

TOTAL: 79 (45%)

OTHER ATTITUDINAL VERBS: enjoy (36); appreciate (6); applaud (5); worship the sun; dread; fear (3); look forward to; miss (4); regret (2); sympathise; believe in; support; despise (2)

TOTAL: 64 (37%)

EMOTIONAL STATES: rejoice (2); suffer

TOTAL: 3 (2%)

MISCELLANEOUS: deserve; excel self; fight; overdrink

TOTAL: 4 (2%)

Ta1   *I en/tīrely*

AGREEING & DISAGREEING: agree (89); disagree (10)

TOTAL: 99 (92%)

MISCELLANEOUS: collapse; owe life to; fall for; forget about; believe; disregard; give self up; approve of; enjoy

TOTAL: 9 (8%)

Ta2   *they /all ūtterly*

DISLIKING: detest (6); dislike (3); abhor (2); loathe (2); hate (10)

TOTAL: 23 (22%)

EXHAUSTION: collapse (6); blank out; tire out; be worn out; exhaust

TOTAL: 10 (10%)

FAILURE TO ATTAIN DESIRABLE GOAL OR STATE: fail (5); despair (4); submit to; give up hope; be confounded; misunderstand; forget

TOTAL: 14 (14%)

OPPOSITION: refuse to (5); deny (3); reject (2); disregard (3); defy; oppose; destroy; rout
TOTAL: 17 (17%)
AGREEING & DISAGREEING: agree (5); disagree (6)
TOTAL: 11 (11%)
OTHER DISAPPROBATORY ATTITUDINAL VERBS: disapprove (2); deplore; despise (5); disdain to; disgust (2); bore (2); drive mad; disbelieve (2); stink
TOTAL: 17 (17%)
MISCELLANEOUS: abandon (2); ignore; disappear (2); vanish; cry out; kill self laughing; enjoy; have a marvellous time; choke on
TOTAL: 11 (11%)

Ta3   *we /all mūch*

LIKING: like (5); love (3); prefer (8); favour
TOTAL: 17 (20%)
WANTING: want to; desire (5); require
TOTAL: 7 (8%)
OTHER APPROBATORY VERBS: admire (25); appreciate (9); enjoy (17); enjoy self
TOTAL: 52 (60%)
MISCELLANEOUS: regret (6); agree (2); concur; fear; abhor; loathe
TOTAL: 12 (14%)
(Doublet: admire and love)

Ta4   *my /friend complētely*

FAILURE TO ATTAIN DESIRABLE GOAL OR STATE: forget (38); fail (3); lose control; give in (2); lose way (2); give up hope; misunderstand (3); lose head; lose nerve; lose hope
TOTAL: 53 (45%)
EXHAUSTION: collapse (2); lose consciousness; faint
TOTAL: 4 (3%)
OPPOSITION: deny (6); reject (3); refuse to; disobey; ruin; overwhelm; disown
TOTAL: 14 (12%)

SURPRISING: astonish (2); baffle (2); surprise; dumbfound
TOTAL: 6 (5%)
MISCELLANEOUS: ignore (16); desert; abandon; agree (4); concur;
   correspond with wish; disappear (3); vanish; finish; waste; abhor; share; fall in love with; trust (2); look the part; run life;
   win over; forgive; dissect
TOTAL: 40 (34%)

Tb1   *my /friend entīrely*

AGREEING & DISAGREEING: agree (38); disagree (6)
TOTAL: 44 (65%)
MISCELLANEOUS: trust (2); believe; take to drugs; need (2); tell;
   depend (up)on (2); surprise; fit the answer; eat; finish; devote
   self; misrepresent; blame self; miss point; abandon; leave; give
   self; like; dislike (2); forget
TOTAL: 24 (35%)

Tb2   *his /father ūtterly*

DISLIKING: detest (6); abhor (2); dislike (2); hate (7); loathe (2)
TOTAL: 19 (28%)
OPPOSITION: condemn (3); forbid (2); refuse to; deny (2); dis-
   regard; cast out (2); ruin; annihilate; kill
TOTAL: 14 (20%)
OTHER DISAPPROBATORY ATTITUDINAL VERBS: despise (7); dis-
   approve (3); revolt; bore
TOTAL: 12 (17%)
MISCELLANEOUS: ignore (2); fail (2); collapse (2); break down;
   lose temper; agree (3); disagree (3); spoil (3); go mad; dis-
   believe; trust; depend upon; mystify; despair; forget
TOTAL: 24 (35%)

Tb3   */some people mūch*

LIKING & DISLIKING: prefer (35); adore (2); like (3); dislike (3);
   hate

TOTAL: 44 (70%)
OTHER APPROBATORY ATTITUDINAL VERBS: admire (11); enjoy (7); desire
TOTAL: 19 (30%)

Tb4   *I com/plētely*

FAILURE TO ATTAIN DESIRABLE GOAL OR STATE: forget (35); fail (3); lose head (2); give up (2); go to pieces; bungle
TOTAL: 44 (63%)
AGREEING & DISAGREEING: agree (5); disagree (4); concur (2)
TOTAL: 11 (16%)
OPPOSITION: refuse; refute; deny (4)
TOTAL: 6 (9%)
MISCELLANEOUS: ignore (2); despise; abhor; trust; surprise self; finish; adore; lose temper
TOTAL: 9 (13%)

BIBLIOGRAPHY

Behre, F. (1967), *Studies in Agatha Christie's Writings* (= *Gothenburg Studies in English* 19) (Göteborg).
Bolinger, D. L. (1961), *Generality, gradience, and the all-or-none* (The Hague).
—— (1969), "Categories, Features, Attributes", *Brno Studies in English* 8.38-41.
Borst, E. (1902), *Die Gradadverbien im Englischen* (= *Anglistische Forschungen*, Heft 10) (Heidelberg).
Chomsky, N. (1965), *Aspects of the Theory of Syntax* (Cambridge, Mass.).
Crystal, D. and Quirk, R. (1964), *Systems of Prosodic and Paralinguistic Features in English* (The Hague).
Firth, J. R. (1957), *Papers in Linguistics 1934-1951* (London).
Greenbaum, S. (1969a), *Studies in English Adverbial Usage* (London).
—— (1969b), "The Question of 'But' ", *Folia Linguistica* III, 3/4.
—— and Quirk, R. (1970), *Elicitation Experiments in English: Linguistic Studies in Use and Attitude* (London).
Gregory, M. (1967), "Aspects of varieties differentiation", *Journal of Linguistics 3*.2, 177-198.
Halliday, M. A. K. (1963), "The Tones of English", *Archivum Linguisticum* 15.1, 1-28.
—— (1966a), "Lexis as a linguistic level", *In Memory of J. R. Firth*, eds. C. E. Bazell *et al.*, 148-162 (London).
—— (1966b), "General Linguistics and its application to language teaching", *Patterns of Language*, eds. A. McIntosh and M. A. K. Halliday, 1-41 (London).
Kirchner, G. (1955), *Gradadverbien: Restriktiva und Verwandtes im heutigen Englisch, Britisch und Amerikanisch* (Halle).
Klima, E. S. (1964), "Negation in English", *The Structure of Language*, eds. J. A. Fodor and J. J. Katz, 246-323 (Englewood Cliffs, New Jersey).
Leech, G. N. (1969), *A Linguistic Guide to English Poetry* (London).
Lyons, J. (1966), "Towards a 'notional' theory of the 'parts of speech' ", *Journal of Linguistics* 2.2, 209-236.
Malkiel, Y. (1966), "Genetic Analysis of Word Formation", *Current Trends in Linguistics* 3, ed. T. A. Sebeok, 305-364 (The Hague).
Matthews, P. H. (1965), "Problems of Selection in Transformational Grammar", *Journal of Linguistics* 1.1, 35-47.

McIntosh, A. (1966), "Patterns and Ranges", *Patterns of Language*, eds. A. McIntosh and M. A. K. Halliday, 183-199 (London).
Mitchell, T. F. (1966), "Some English Phrasal Types", *In Memory of J. R. Firth*, eds. C. E. Bazell *et al.*, 335-358 (London).
Quirk, R. (1960), "Towards a Description of English Usage", *Transactions of the Philological Society*, 40-61 (Oxford).
—— (1965), "Descriptive Statement and Serial Relationship", *Language* 41, 205-217.
—— and Svartvik, J. (1966), *Investigating Linguistic Acceptability* (The Hague).
Sinclair, J. McH. (1966), "Beginning the study of lexis", *In Memory of J. R. Firth*, eds. C. E. Bazell *et al.*, 410-430 (London).
Spitzbardt, H. (1965), "English Adverbs of Degree and their Semantic Fields", *Philologica Pragensia* 8, 349-359.
Stoffel, C. (1901), *Intensives and Down-toners* (= *Anglistische Forschungen*, Heft 1) (Heidelberg).
Svartvik, J. (1966), *On Voice in the English Verb* (The Hague).
—— (1968), "Plotting Divided Usage with *Dare* and *Need*", *Studia Neophilologica* 40.1, 130-140.
Thorndike, E. L. and Lorge, I. (1944), *The Teacher's Word Book of 30,000 Words* (New York).
Zimmer, K. E. (1964), *Affixal Negation in English and Other Languages* (= *Supplement to Word* 20.2, Monograph 5).

JANUA LINGUARUM

STUDIA MEMORIAE NICOLAI VAN WIJK DEDICATA

Edited by C. H. van Schooneveld

SERIES MINOR